Facilitating Active Learning

FREEDOM TO ENGAGE

A critical auto-ethnographic analysis of an action research project

BY MICHELLE RHNEA YISRAEL

A critical auto-ethnographic analysis of a community college professor

Freedom to E.N.G.A.G.E.

Exercise
Nurture
Grade
Action
Genuineness
Exchange

Published by I AM Media Books
All Rights Reserved © 2020

Freedom to ENGAGE © 2020 Michelle R. Yisrael
Editing and Interior Layout by: The Words Doctors

All rights reserved under International and Pan-American Copyright Conventions.

No part of this publication may be reproduced in whole or in part, or stored in a retrieval system, or transmitted in any form or by any means, electronic, mechanical, photocopying, recording, or otherwise, without written permission of the author.

ISBN: 978-1-951667-13-9
Published by I AM Media Books, Michigan, USA
Media to Awaken the World!

www.iammediabooks.com

Table of Contents

1. Who are the at-risk? Why?
2. Inquiry-Based Learning
3. Restorative Practices
4. How I Prepare to Teach
5. Technology in the Classroom
6. Critical Relationships
7. Managing Counterproductive Behavior - A Study
8. Reflective Teaching & Learning
9. E.N.G.A.G.E. Action Plan
10. Case Studies
11. Educator's Growth Plan
12. References

1

Who is at risk? Why?

The United States is facing a literacy crisis. More than 30 million adults in the United States cannot read, write, or do basic math above a third-grade level. Many of these adults attended kindergarten through 12th grade, yet still, they remain not literate. Children whose parents possess low literacy levels have a 72 percent chance of reading at the lowest levels themselves. These children are more likely to get poor grades, display behavioral problems, exhibit high absentee rates, repeat school years, or drop out according to the National Bureau of Economic Research (NBER). Many of these poor performing children are children of color, from rural and urban areas. *The Rand Report: Evaluating the Effectiveness of Correctional Education* estimates 75 percent of state prison inmates did not complete high school, or can be classified as low literate. Again, these are people of color and a strong cause for hopelessness in this field of study.

We know mass incarceration disproportionately impacts Black and Brown people, and many of these people incarcerated are again, people of color. The *American Journal of Public Health* contends low literacy contributes to over $230 billion a year in health care costs, because almost half of Americans cannot read well enough to comprehend health information, which results in incurring higher costs. Again, people of color. Literacy represents power; this is why slave owners kept their slaves illiterate. Illiteracy perpetuated powerlessness in slaves; thereby ensuring the slave owners would remain in power. Frederick Douglas asserted, *"Once you learn to read, you will be forever free."* Thus, according to readily available statistics, freedom for people of color is stripped away because of illiteracy.

We spend too much time trying to prove racism still exists in school systems across the country and analyzing statistics regarding the impacts of the education of races in America upon social justice. Upon careful and thorough scrutiny, we find evidence to support the claim that the education system in America is still racist and segregated. Furthermore, we discover educational equity and 21st-century social justice maintain a status quo which is intolerant, biased, and prejudiced. The data proves these facts so many try to deny. Literacy numbers and school success rates make it clear. Anyone researching the US Department of Education and the US Census Bureau can find these numbers on the internet. These statistics can serve as impediments to teaching causing educators to feel hopeless.

According to the NAACP, African Americans are incarcerated at more than 5 times the rate of whites, and the imprisonment rate for African American women is twice that of white women. Moreover, it is becoming common knowledge that though African Americans and Hispanics make up approximately 32% of the US population, they comprised 56% of all incarcerated people in 2015. The *NAACP Fair Chance Hiring Fact Sheet* reports an even more disheartening statistic: *"nationwide, African American children represent 32% of children who are arrested, 42% of children who are detained, and 52% of children whose cases are judicially waived to criminal court."*

As a result of the rising at-risk population of marginalized youth, we are faced with a nationwide epidemic of young black males finding themselves trekking from juvenile to adulthood through the prison pipeline in astronomical numbers. References to the impact of the prison pipeline appear in multiple media formats, including Netflix's *13th Documentary*, as well as the text, *The New Jim Crow* by Michelle Alexander. Similarly, throughout the history of educational reform, little, if any attention has been placed specifically on the educational welfare and wellbeing of the black male child. Prior to education reform during the 1970s, focused on young black children, this kind of history in the classroom was nonexistent. Today, however, history is repeating itself and culturally relevant history in the classroom has been phased out over a period of time. As veteran educators, surely we can remember when a black history curriculum was unheard of in educational arenas nationwide.

It is imperative for educators to be cognizant, not only of the needs of young black males as a marginalized group within the at-risk population, but also understand the barriers that impact the student population they serve and not see this population as an impediment. Instead, this is an opportunity to look at this population of students, and all marginalized subsets, as students with promise. Educators come from diverse backgrounds; they may or may not have experienced marginalization in the same manner as the students in their classrooms. As a result, many educators may find it difficult to succeed outside their comfort zone without the proper proficiencies and tools. For example, Black youth, most significantly males in as early as third and fourth grades, are targeted due to "at risk" behaviors, coupled with environmental, and socio-economic conditions that have thwarted their perceptual views of learning and social interactions.

Teachers from inner city schools can look up their previous students who were pushed through the system by social promotions, suffered severe behavior problems, or those who graduated without adequate literacy skills, and see 90% of them either died from violence or had issues in the criminal justice system. Our classrooms served as direct pipelines to mass incarceration. We need to shift our focus from getting through the day to ensuring our students gain skill and learn concepts. Administration needs to give teachers in elementary and secondary schools the freedom to creatively engage our students. As we watch our government allocate money to national defense and prisons, I hope they decide to push more of that money into education. Education comes from the same pocket as social programs and training. I want education to have its own bucket.

At the same time, teachers should do better about how we make our students feel about school and learning. Unfortunately, some teachers call students stupid or ignorant. Other teachers tell students they are not college material, or they will never amount to anything. Rarely do teachers and administrators seek to understand students with behavior issues, find out why they behave the way they do, or even offer suggestions and strategies to combat that behavior so they can learn. In good conscious, teachers need to reflect on our own thoughts and behaviors regarding our students, and assess our expectations of them, and either fully engage ourselves in our students' success, or decide to find another career if we cannot do it. Teachers need to engage students in learning. Our best students will learn whether we engage them or not. They will learn sitting in the park under a tree, we just need to be consistent with them. It is difficult to reach students who need our focus, attention, and more specialized resources than we possess.

Teachers must serve as "spring-boards", or the first line of defense, to establish best practices for educating this targeted population. An educator's call to arms will require moving beyond "bedside" manners, pedagogical strategies, and methodologies and fully engaging ourselves, along with nurturing our empathic abilities to acquire an in-depth look into the inner "soul" of the child. The educator must develop a holistic approach to teaching by first, undergoing critical self-reflection to understand who he or she is as the lead change agent in the classroom. In order to reach the at-risk child, the self-reflective teacher must put him or herself in a position to develop a working relationship with each student. This relationship will prompt the reflective educator to take a realistic look in the mirror and ask: *"How do I move beyond mere pedagogical understanding to achieve practical proficiency?"* As my student's first line of defense, this poses an important question. While society and administrators focus on test scores and completion rates, I need to focus on how I can teach, while encouraging my students to learn.

To meet the needs of 21st Century learners, educators must understand their language, which only translates through *"affective communication"*. The operative word is *"affective"*, in contrast to *"effective"* communication. *"Affective"* communication focuses on feelings and emotions, unlike *"effective"* communication, which focuses on delivery and predefined metrics. The 21st Century learner wants to know *"Can you feel me?"*, and not *"Do you understand me?"* Therefore, today's educators must learn how to communicate *"affectively"*, and move beyond effective communication alone. We need to concern ourselves with our student's struggles, and their level of grit.

Helping students shift from a fixed mindset to a growth mindset is important. Being concerned with their emotional intelligence is now important, since many at-risk youths have a big ball of negative emotion which distracts them from learning. This population's language, spawned from *"in-affective"* communication, brought on by social ills, historical backlash, fears, violence, pain, distrust, perceptions, beliefs, etc., etc., etc., further widens the gap between educators and 21st Century learners. These descriptors identify a direct linkage between mass incarceration and the school to prison pipeline, where poverty provides a direct link to illiteracy.

The achievement gap continues to widen. Black children's dropout rates continue to increase, while their reading levels fall far below those of White children. It has to stop. The statistics and the playing field need to be leveled. How is it possible that Black youth attend 13 years of schooling, from kindergarten to 12th grade, and still graduate with literacy issues? Julian Bond observed, *"Violence is black children going to school for 12 years and receiving 6 years' worth of education."* Who else is tired of this criminal level of violence to our community's children, which has become accepted as normal? Whose responsibility is it to change the facts our youth face? No one of us can change this racist educational system. We need all hands on deck; each parent, educator, counselor and support staff personnel doing what they are responsible for in a better way. How then, does this look for you? What can you do?

Why are they at risk?

In 1955, author Rudolf Flesch wrote the bestselling book *Why Johnny Can't Read*, where he investigated how reading was taught in the United States. The problems persist today. Too many of our children still don't get the kind of instruction they need to excel. As a result, our nation's dropout rates rise faster than our graduation rates. Why? Firstly, growing numbers of our youth are allowed to graduate high school, even though they lack sufficient literacy skills to serve as productive members of society. Secondly, high school dropouts from families who do not endeavor to improve their economic status, typically produce children of parents who drop out as well. Thirdly, our youth not only dropout of high school, they also drop off the educational grid in seventh and eighth grade in growing numbers. The National Center for Education Statistics estimates thousands of children do not make it past eighth grade. Finally, students jump into their first-year college experience unprepared for college-level courses. Colleges are then expected to remediate and retain students who lack the basic skills necessary for success. These impediments to teaching cause professors to feel helpless and hopeless in districts nationwide.

The California Department of Education reported 3.5% of eighth-graders, 17,257 in all, never returned for their ninth-grade year in 2011. It is conceivable that these families created inadequate literate behavior in their children. Without further education and training these parents will become so rooted in their own deficiencies and poverty-stricken lifestyle, they will fail to address the growing needs of their children. For this reason, the cycle of illiteracy poses a difficult barrier to break. Adolescence is a terrible time to become trapped in hopelessness, but many students never overcome these challenges because they lack the support they need to succeed. According to a 2005 drop out report, in the state of Illinois alone, approximately 12,871 students between the ages of 13-21 dropped out of school. In a 2016 National Public Radio report the state of Alabama admitted inflated the high school graduation rates provided to the National Center for Education Statistics. The city of Atlanta reports graduation rates at 46.8%. Does that mean the dropout rate is 53.2%? The official state of Michigan website reports from 2012-2016, high school graduation rates remained in the 79% range, falling only slightly.

The Illinois State Board of Education's 2018 report card stated in 2018 nearly 20% fewer Blacks than Whites graduated from high school. The report estimated similar stats for low-income youth. Further, the report predicted more females, Black or White, will graduate than males. In addition, the same report estimated Hispanics are more likely to graduate high school than Blacks, but less likely than Whites. These statistics, and the statistics for all states, are openly available. Use the internet to conduct a simple Google search for your state's dropout and graduation rates. You will discover, in the words of the ill-fated Apollo 13 mission: *"Houston, we have a problem!"* Clearly this problem impacts all of us! I actively engage these students for first the time in my developmental English courses at the community college where I teach, and I am often their first, and only, line of defense between academic failure and success.

The number of *"Johnnie's"* who cannot read has grown exponentially, due to a discouraged, unmotivated, and invading populace with fixed mindsets, ill-prepared for growth. Clearly, America has suffered from education problems for generations, resulting in often ignored youth disrupting classrooms. Many educators lack the expertise, resources, and support to engage students and equip them to overcome the barriers to academic achievement. This is no time for excuses, we need action. Students need educators who actively engage them in learning.

"Do you know that there are no remedial reading cases in Austrian schools? Do you know that there are no remedial reading cases in Germany, in France, in Italy, in Norway, in Spain — practically anywhere in the world except in the United States? Do you know that there was no such thing as remedial reading in this country either until about thirty years ago? Do you know that the teaching of reading never was a problem anywhere in the world until the United States switched to the present method around about 1925?" Why Johnny Can't Read? And What You Can Do About It (Rudolf Flesch 1955).

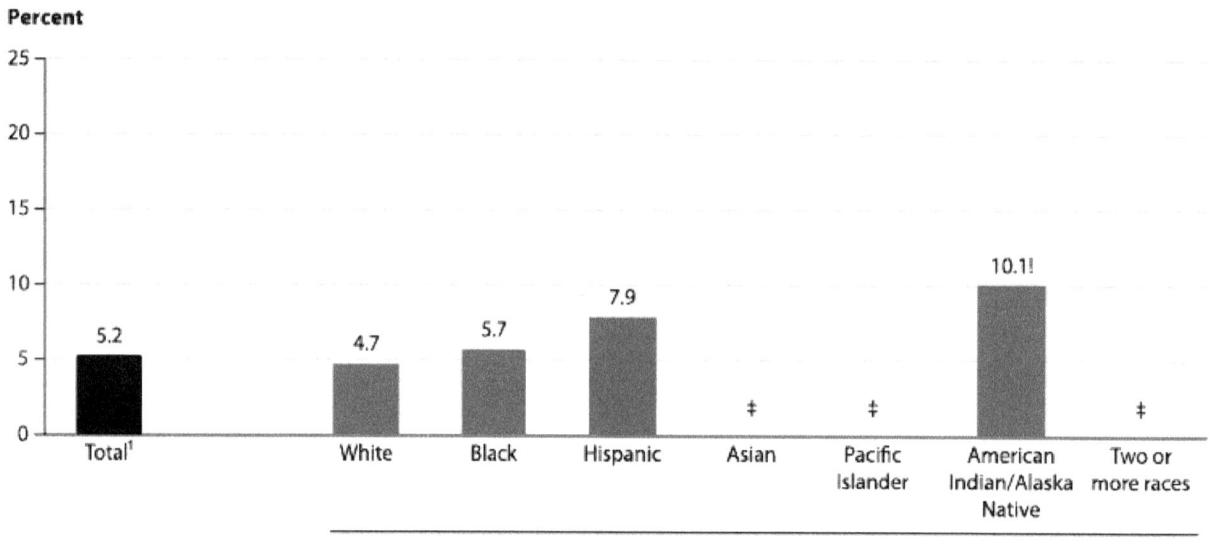

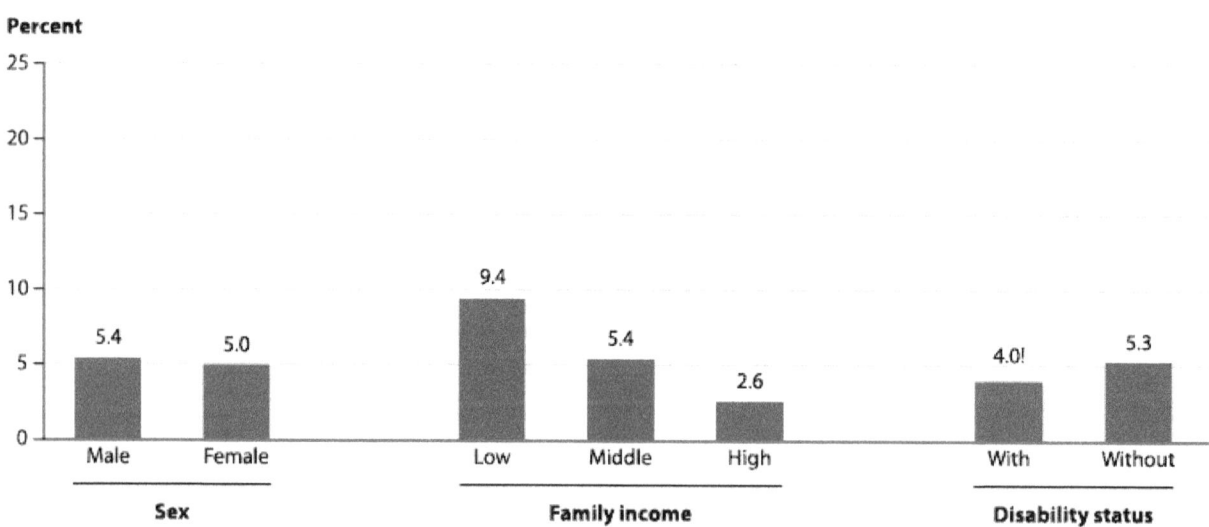

! Interpret data with caution. The coefficient of variation (CV) for this estimate is between 30 and 50 percent.
‡ Reporting standards not met. Either there are too few cases for a reliable estimate or the coefficient of variation (CV) is 50 percent or greater.
[1] Includes other racial/ethnic categories not separately shown.
NOTE: The event dropout rate is the percentage of 15- to 24-year-olds who dropped out of grades 10–12 between one October and the next (e.g., October 2013 to October 2014). Dropping out is defined as leaving school without a high school diploma or alternative credential, such as a GED certificate. Race categories exclude persons of Hispanic ethnicity. Low income is defined as the bottom 20 percent of all family incomes; middle income is between 20 and 80 percent of all family incomes, and high income is the top 20 percent of all family incomes. In 2014, low income was defined as $19,716 or less, and high income was defined as $95,433 or more. Individuals identified as having a disability reported difficulty in at least one of the following: hearing, seeing even when wearing glasses, walking or climbing stairs, dressing or bathing, doing errands alone, concentrating, remembering, or making decisions. Data are based on sample surveys of the civilian noninstitutionalized population.
SOURCE: U.S. Department of Commerce, Census Bureau, Current Population Survey (CPS), October 2014. See table 1.1.

The term literacy has become a favorite topic for educators and politicians. *"Literacy is an individual's ability to read, write, and speak in English; compute and solve problems at levels of proficiency necessary to function on the job and in society; to achieve one's goals and develop one's knowledge and potential."* (NIFL, April 2000) Close to 30% of the American population over age sixteen suffer from profound literacy deficiencies. This means millions of people lack adequate reading, writing, and critical thinking skills necessary for proper survival.

According to the National Institute for Literacy, poverty and literacy are directly linked. Statistics show more lower-income level students drop out of school than students at higher income levels. Additionally, the reading and writing levels of young people are closely related to the educational levels of their parents. Literacy has also been linked to increased civil behavior, the inability to formulate higher levels of thought in problem-solving skills, and knowledge that creates the resources necessary for civil obedience. It is 2020, and nothing has changed. As a matter of fact, when you read the news and examine grades and test scores of our young people, it seems as though our prospects for academic success have gotten much worse.

Society, particularly politicians, do not make the education of our youth a priority. We know this because the politicians pull the purse strings. We see where our tax dollars are being spent, and not spent. We read about cutbacks and fiscal responsibility, and education always suffers when politicians make decisions to cut social programs. Political leaders have been known to hold the release of budgetary funds that impact the education of our youth. Not only are schools being closed down because of a lack of funding, they are also being closed down because teachers lack the resources to properly engage their students. As a result, students fail to achieve, and many are actually illiterate, even in high school. The NAACP Fact Sheet observed literacy rates rose until the 1980's, but after that period rates began to dip slightly.

Facing the problem

There are many impediments to freedom to engage students in real learning. Some are systematic others are created by teachers out of fear and lack of training. Classroom management is typically missing from most university programs. Teachers are expected to gain this skill in the student teaching and practicum phase, many don't. One of the first things we need to do as educators is not to look at our students as at-risk but as students with promise. We need to raise our expectations and figure out how to regain a passion for what we do since students are inspired by our passion or discouraged because of our lack of it. Our passion and ability to inspire these students ``with promise" becomes a remedy to combat negative impediments to teaching and learning. If I do not expect my students to reach the goals of the learning, they will not reach them. If my expectations are low, theirs will remain low as well. Therefore, in facing the problem, my disposition becomes either an impediment or motivation.

If I allow my students to feel it when I am overwhelmed or feeling hopeless, it affects their ability to learn what I am attempting to teach. It is imperative for me to maintain a positive attitude because doing so improves my ability to help students learn and understand the lessons and material I need to teach them. My disposition is crucial. It is imperative that I set the atmosphere for learning on the very first day and continue the first two weeks of the semester. The two-week orientation is when I set a positive atmosphere by explaining your expectations to the students and setting up small successes as learning is emotional and the way I set up the learning environment has to stir emotion.

Emotions are vital to patterns of failure. The students with promise enrolled in my developmental English courses are usually afraid of writing and very discouraged by it. My goal is to tear down these walls and the first two weeks are important to the process. Whenever a student learns something or fails at a task, there is always an emotional response. One of the strongest implications of brain-based learning is that every decision has some kind of emotion linked to it so that, a classroom is an emotional place. This is considered one of the strongest implications of brain-based learning. My students must feel respected, my disposition speaks to them, in order to build the environment necessary to help them succeed.

Because I know a body that has enough water and good food is the body more open for the brain to learn, I never restrict my students from getting up going to the water fountain or getting themselves a snack. And yes, they are free to bring their snacks, a meal, and drinks to the classroom. The choices they bring back is sometimes a teachable moment about health and wellness and how the brain functions. The literature says brain fuel is increased with a combination of water, oxygen, glucose. *"The human brain consumes 20% of the body's calories and needs a constant supply of water, oxygen, and glucose to function at optimal levels. The lack of any one of these can significantly affect a student's learning, but when balanced properly can improve working memory, attention, and motor functions."* (Jensen & McConchie, 2020, p. 25).

Moreover, I begin the action research process on day one, taking mental and physical notes of students' responses to my methods and to the environment. Action research is a study carried out by an educator in the course of his or her activity used to improve the methods and approach of his or her own instructional practices to both improve both teaching and learning. Action research is linked to a critical reflection that has proven to be a powerful experience. It has helped me become more effective at one of the things I care a lot about, the growth and development of my students. The countless hours I spend reflecting on my practices have made a real difference in my students' lives and makes me understand I am doing the right thing with my life. I make a difference and what I do endlessly is worthwhile.

Our educational system has far too many learning theories and far too many academic research monies, time and energy have been put into the research. In recent decades, elementary and secondary school teachers have been expected to focus on testing and test-taking skills. They have not been free to be creative in their teaching methods so they can involve themselves in action research reflecting on their instructional practices and collaborating on these practices.

We need more action research, not learning theories. We can begin in your own workplace. We can start small and keep track of our results. We can then take this information to the public, which is what I am doing with this *Freedom to ENGAGE* book. We can let our students in on what we're doing which is what I have done each semester. We can talk to them about the brain and how we learn, which I incorporate into lectures and activities as often as possible when appropriate. And we can make sure other faculty and staff members know about the information. Making minority history part of American history, we connect national history to local and contemporary history as well. This way, students have ample time to become familiar with lesser known historians that they may not learn about in one month as teachers tend to design projects and lessons about the famous folk.

Unfortunately, parents, counselors, social workers, behavior management staff, and educators today must also serve as social justice advocates. Our youth need all hands on deck. Today's students are more likely to be in larger classes where they receive less individualized attention and fewer opportunities to survey their own particular passions and interests. Keeping in mind, teachers as the instructional leaders in the classroom must hone pedagogical skills to ensure student achievement. In doing so, educators are able to ensure students' needs are differentiated as well as met. Furthermore, teachers must have the opportunity and support from their administration that allows them the time and resources to plan instruction. In planning, they have the ability to prevent challenges in classroom management and foster rigor and engagement.

The elephant in the room is the lack of funding and public support (e.g., political, administrative, and parental). As a result, teachers are not able to take a strategic approach to plan for teaching. Astute teachers want to be creative in their teaching, engage students with rigor and relevance but are being distracted by continual educational reform mandates. It is in our experience that, in making every minute count, challenges in the classroom are prevented. At the institution where I currently teach, the course our students enjoy the most is Africana Studies 101. This tells me that students want to study issues relating to themselves of past and present. It also says we should be celebrating Black accomplishments and infusing Black history into our courses throughout the year.

Black history being taught in isolation, one month a year, tells Black students they are not important. I will similarly argue for infusing Women's Studies, Latino History, Native American History, and Asian History into the yearly curriculum instead of giving these minorities only one month of focus. Teaching these histories in silo gives the same message, minority people are less important than the majority. We can encourage our students to become changes agents by creating year-wide projects relating to issues they care about and encouraging them to create actionable projects and deliverables to persuade and advocate for minorities and social justice issues. They want to change and they are good at motivating others to change as well. These types of projects help our students connect Black History to the history of other minorities.

Moreover, it removes Black History from the past, reinforces the fact that Black History happens every day, and invites students to conceptualize the idea that "they" are making history as well.

Building a professional and trusting relationship between teacher and student is tantamount in restructuring a learning environment that is governed by collaboration, effective communication, emotional awareness, relevant and sustainable learning while making every minute count. Relationship building exemplifies the essential components in changing the direction of today's educational system. As educators, we believe the "whole child" approach best governs the decision-making process which is supported by restorative practices. Foremost, we understand educators must undertake a mindset of ownership to the wellbeing and welfare of the students they serve. With that being said, though everything changes and nothing stays the same, we must remain steadfast in the fight against the variables that have been essential in dismantling capabilities and resources. In doing so, we further the empowerment of our students within and beyond the educational arena.

I questioned both education in my city and the educational process, because of my own educational experience. Since I was not impressed by the education I received, I knew I wanted something different as well as more, for my own children. I only remember having three great teachers in elementary school. These effective teachers transformed me in 5th grade, 6th grade, and 8th grade. Though my high school rank was 128 out of over 1500 students, I never understood why I ranked so high. I honestly did not learn anything in high school, except how to type 60 words a minute. I was an avid reader, so I valued education because of the things I learned through my personal reading. Because I lived an alternative lifestyle, as our children grew into school-age, homeschooling was natural for our family and our only recourse. My failed educational experience in public schools helped me realize I wanted more for my children.

I lived an alternative lifestyle that was contrary to the norm on the southside of Chicago while a young woman. I lived in the 'hood' as a newly married wife. My children were born-at-home, we were more healthy-eaters than our families and friends, and we homeschooled our children. We introduced them to words early. I read to them daily, from birth. I posted words around the house and labeled household items. We didn't watch much television in those days, and the internet had yet to be invented. Books and board games were a part of our lives. My oldest daughter read fluently by the age of 4. Though my oldest son preferred to play ball outside with his friends, he was required to read at least an hour a day before he went out. I wanted my children to be more prepared than their peers.

When family and friends saw how well my children were progressing, they wanted me to teach their children as well. Before I knew what was happening, I had 12 children of various ages in my little one-room schoolhouse, housed on my enclosed back porch. I taught little people how to read and formulate their ideas in a simple 3 sentence paragraph by age 4. Their little sentences had a subject and verb and as I think back on them, they were so cute. When I got them in our school young and eager, this was so much simpler and so quick. I did not even need many resources; a chalkboard, lined and unlined paper, crayons, markers, colored pencils, magazine pictures, a few cardboard boxes, a bin full of a variety of empty tops and bottles from my kitchen, a jumbo pencil each little person could easily hold, a set of blunt scissors for each of my babies, a set of rhythm sticks for each student, and my drum, my shakore', and a box of toys were a good start.

I began my trek with homeschooling, which then birthed of one of three independent schools on the southside of Chicago. Brother Hannibal Afrik and Sister Folami from Shu la Ya Watoto from the westside of Chicago were very helpful in helping me develop my educational framework and precepts for educating the children in my charge. They became my mentors. They allowed me to observe classes through clinical observations and gave me personalized training. Brother Hannibal and Sister Folami walked through my 'one-room schoolhouse' and gave me constructive feedback on my practices through modeling and discussion. They were my teachers before my formal pedagogical training began.

What started off as a personal choice to homeschool my own children soon gave birth to The Israel Academy, which flourished for the first 17 years of my career in education. I founded my own school, directed an alternative high school, and supervised instruction. I also conducted professional development and behavior management workshops for administrators, teachers, security, and other support staff for a network of 8 alternative high schools. Over the past 36 years, I have taught each level from pre-K through high school. I taught reading and writing to the primary and elementary school, where students are happy, eager to learn and eager to please. Later, I taught middle school, where students had become discouraged and were, sometimes, levels behind their peers. They learned to literally hate school because of their experiences in somebody's classroom. I have taught in high school programs where students have literally been dumped, academically abused, and near the age out phase where public schools are no longer responsible for them. What I learned from my experience is students not only want, they need educators to engage them.

2
Inquiry-Based Learning

Lectures provide the least effective way to transfer information; however, I use Inquiry-based learning to introduce some and/or reacquaint many of my students with the joys of learning. Inquiry-based learning is a form of active learning. It starts by posing questions, problems or scenarios, in contrast with traditional education, which generally relies on the teacher presenting facts and his or her knowledge about the subject. Inquiry-based learning often utilizes a facilitator, rather than a lecturer. Through my studies and reflection on my own teaching and learning practices, I understood inquiry-based instruction as a unique, student-centered, skilled instructional method. Inquiry-based instruction leads students to increase their understanding of the process of solving a problem in a creative and authentic manner while meeting the required common core standards. Inquiry-based learning also assists students with social, emotional, and academic developmental issues by allowing students to use their skills which they feel are best developed.

The literature supports inquiry-based learning as an active learning and an effective strategy for student learning gains in a college classroom. Students involved in the traditional lectures were found to be more likely to fail as compared to those in classes with substantial active learning. What does it look like in a classroom? In a course where active learning exists, students vigorously engage in the learning process. Students might collaborate with the course material and grapple with problems of the discipline, or generate questions about the material. In a course where active learning exists students constantly process what they read and learn.

Students may watch a video, look at PowerPoint slides, or share research; however, they are also discussing or debating questions posed by the instructor and are analyzing the information presented to them critically. The instructor may ask students to use their phones to search the Internet to look for data and resources to support their arguments. As the instructor facilitates learning, she exposes students to an extensive amount of material both inside and outside of the call. In class, time is devoted to hands-on learning and sharing information in small groups. In order to facilitate learning in this manner, time and creativity must be reflected upon to achieve the full benefits and increase student learning. Although, active learning can easily and effectively be incorporated into classrooms without the need for a huge overhauling of the course. I find that reflecting on my own practice to identify areas in which active learning could be used, and identifying strategies already being used that can be built upon, is time well spent. The projects I create are complex but not too difficult to achieve and complete.

In my experience, teaching has become a multifaceted process where the teacher has many student learning objectives that must be included in their day-to-day school functions and operations. This includes testing pressures, short class periods, compartmentalized subjects, increased class sizes, conflicts as well as other days to disruptions. Inquiry-based instruction is an effective teaching and learning strategy for educating the whole-child; or the whole-student. As I learned to increase my abilities to create, implement and assess inquiry-based instruction, I provided my students a foundation to establish collaboration and negotiation skills, while working in a group setting. As a constructivist educator, I asked one big question, then provided students with time to think about the question, and led them to the resources for the answer to the questions. I assessed the students' skills while fostering the academic standards based on the project's student-generated design and focus. Inquiry-based instruction and the project should build on the student's prior knowledge as well as the development of scientific-inquiry methods. *"Tell me and I forget. Teach me and I remember. Involve me and I learn."* Benjamin Franklin

Inquiry-based learning is supported by the constructivist learning theory, which asserts *"learning"* occurs within a social context. The idea is people learn from one another, through observation, imitation, and modeling. The constructivist learning theory further establishes: *"learning is a social activity"* and contends *"students learn by doing."* Students learn as they experience and connect their learning to prior knowledge. Constructivism combines the collaboration and evolution of the theories of John Dewey, Jean Piaget, Jerome Bruner, and Levi Vygotsky. According to the Merriam Webster dictionary, epistemology is *the study or a theory of the nature and grounds of knowledge especially with reference to its limits and validity.*

Constructivism finds its roots in epistemology, because there is no single valid methodology from which learning happens. Rather learning entails philosophical, educational, as well as social theories. Moreover, when learning occurs by doing, students' self-efficacy expands because learning serves as a conduit for students to foster positive relationships with others. Lessons learned from inquiry-based learning motivate students because they meet Maslow's hierarchy of needs. As a result, students make connections to a theoretical approach as learning relates to their everyday lives. In this context, learning engages and it stimulates students' curiosity while permitting them to express their creativity. In *Strengthening Student Engagement: What Do Students Want,* Silver, Strong and Robinson (1995) identified five goals which energize students who engage in their work called SCORE:

- **S**uccess (the need for mastery)
- **C**uriosity (the need for understanding)
- **O**riginality (the need for self-expression)
- **R**elationship (the need for involvement with others)
- **E**nergy (to complete the task-extrinsic and intrinsic motivation)

This acronym about engaging students caused a reflective educator to rethink what motivates students, causes a redevelopment of learning goals, and makes them more relevant. Thus, "score" serves as a metaphor for performance, allowing extrinsic motivation to align with intrinsic motivation. This arouses students' curiosity and invites them to succeed as they make small accomplishments, one at a time, step by step, as the project develops. Moreover, learning begins from the top of the cognitive domain of Bloom's Taxonomy and moves down the pyramid from creating to remembering, rather than from remembering where learning takes longer and proves less effective.

Consequently, inquiry-based lessons should work on two levels:
- One level should provide an internal understanding, which leads to changes in one's beliefs, attitudes, or skills (Scardamalia & Bereiter, 2003).

- The second level should focus on knowledge-building, which leads to creating new cognitive artifacts as the results of common goals, group discussions, and synthesis.

I rarely assign a project the same way. Each time I decide to assign a project I previously assigned, I make adjustments and revisions to the instructions and/or the deliverables. Based on the students and their way of thinking, the outcome is rarely consistent, though the learning is. I measure students' level of engagement based upon their excitement. Engaged students don't appear to mind doing the work and exhibit excitement about it. Another sign of engagement is when students persist and struggle through challenges, while asking questions and answering questions for one another when they can; so learning becomes a communal experience. Consequently, my learning as an educator continues; I learn to create effective projects composed of three major components:

1. Relevancy, clear goals and or purpose. Keeping in mind the academic standards, the desired higher-order thinking skills and what the students will produce or accomplish should establish the project's design and the method of investigation and evaluation.

2. Student-generated ideas, interest, questions, or needs should drive the project design. Allowing for an inquiry to be relevant to real-life and real-life solutions; new perspectives and information will lead to discovering a variety of answers, rather than "only" one correct answer. In this part of the project, the instructor assists in developing curriculum-framing questions based on the decision of the type of project or issues, as well as the assessment plan (check-ins; rubrics; reflective writing).

3. Design activities needed to illustrate the mastery of knowledge and skills demonstrated through authentic products or performances. This is the result of collaborative inquiry, and coaching from the teacher who serves as the facilitator of discussion and questioning. All collective parts work within the concept of collective leadership where everyone maintains a vital position or portion in the development and completion of the project.

In my role as an inquiry-based educator, I:
- Develop projects which increase critical thinking
- Facilitate learning in the classroom
- Encourage critical response writing in each subject I teach
- Encourage my students to understand their learning styles
- Pre-assess student skill levels
- Implement projects from beginning to completion
- Apply formative assessment techniques to enforce understanding
- Create effective rubrics as summative assessment projects and major assignments.

The learner benefits:
- Allows for in-depth investigation
- Generates driving questions or challenges and debates- creating a need to know;
- Encourages innovation while giving students a voice and choice
- Compromises with teammates
- Creates methods of developing a personally meaningful artifact
- Develops critiquing & revision skills
- Encourages self-evaluation
- Increases 21st Century Skills

Approaches to Inquiry-Based Instruction

Various approaches exist for instructional utilization to assist the different learning styles of the learners. By trial and error, I experimented with a variety of learning style assessment tools to assist in the academic success of my students. Inquiry-Based Learning is similar to Problem-Based Learning and Experiential learning. All three are greatly influenced by Brain-Based Learning, which moves student skills down Bloom's Taxonomy from synthesizing and creating to knowledge and remembering rather than the other way around. This movement down the pyramid causes active and deep learning. It also invites students to identify and sharpen their metacognitive awareness while they solve problems, which results in them owning their learning. Learning is complex, rather than difficult. Therefore, deep learning increases, learning challenges, cognitive growth occurs, and higher-order thinking occurs organically. All three can develop a versatile curriculum and facilitate the various learning styles of the population.

Problem-Based Instruction is a student-centered pedagogy where students learn about a subject through the experience of solving an open-ended problem. Students learn thinking strategies and domain knowledge. Problem-Based Instruction, Understanding by Design (UBD) or Backward Design are all subsets of Inquiry-Based Instruction.

Problem-Based Learning (PBL) vs **Inquiry-Based Instruction (IBI)**

Similarities	Differences
Focuses on open-minded questions & tasks	**IBI** tending to take weeks or months to complete. **PBL** tends to embed shorter completion times.
It provides authentic opportunities to differentiate the content, context, process, product, environment, and skills learned.	**IBI** is often interdisciplinary. **PBL** is usually about a single subject.
Allows students to be independent learners & empowers students for 21st Century learning	**IBI** usually includes the creation of a product, publication, or performance. **PBL** the product is more often proposed for a solution to the problem expressed in a publication.
Emphasizes student inquiry & includes multi-faceted learning opportunities.	**IBI** is more often based on a real-life and authentic task but could be a real scenario. **PBL** uses case studies or fictitious scenarios as structured problems but could be real.

Backward Design Learning (BDL)

Backward Design Learning has been listed as a method of designing an educational curriculum in three stages. It is used as a means of setting goals before choosing an instructional method and various forms of assessments. Backward Design Learning is like a "Roadmap" to learning and a method to teach toward the "End Point" or learning goal (Wiggins & McTighe, 2008, pp. 17-18). Backward Design Learning theory exists in 3 stages. *"In stage 1 we consider our goals, examine established content standards (national, state, district), and review curriculum expectations"* (18). In stage 2 we determine what *"collected evidence [is] needed to document and validate that the desired learning has been achieved"* (18). Finally, in stage 3 we determine *"appropriate instructional activities"* (18). Learning experiences and instruction (17-18) are mapped and well planned.

1. **Big Ideas and or Skills** – *"identify the results desired."*
    a. Focus on the "Big Ideas" (principles, theories, concepts, point of views, or theme)
    b. What should the students know, understand, and be able to do?
    c. Consider the goals and expectations of the curriculum.
2. **Determine the level of evidence** (acceptable evidence) that supports the desired results which have occurred. Determine the methods and evidence which will demonstrate an understanding of what has taken place, (culminating assessment tasks and range of assessment methods). Observations, tests, and or projects can be used.

3. **Map and design activities that make the desired results happen.** What knowledge and skills will my students need to achieve the desired result? As if creating a map of necessary steps, I consider teaching methods, sequences of lessons, formative assessments, and resource materials needed for the desired outcome. What plans will I need to put in place to ensure my students gain the skills necessary to meet the desired outcome and solve the problems, complete the project, or develop a presentation? What guidance will students need to actually learn what they were expected to learn? How will I create the course and its modules so they are focused on the student learning outcome, rather than my teaching process?

The goal of my development English course is to simultaneously build reading comprehension skills and teach students to write a 5-paragraph college essay in 16 weeks. This is stage one, the big idea. When students are successful, they complete and understand a particular outcome. Looking at this daunting task backward is less of a challenge when using the three steps of Understanding by Design (UbD). First, I need to develop a relationship with students and have them trust me and my process. They need to know I believe in them and I will not leave them to do this work alone. They also need to know they can rely on one another to get us to where we need to go. The Campus Scavenger Hunt and Syllabus Scavenger Hunt are the tools I use to do it. Then, I need to be upfront with them regarding the daunting task ahead of us by showing them it can be done and they are the ones who can do it. I use a copy of an essay written by a previous student for this purpose. We conduct a slow and thorough analysis of the essay using the carefully crafted rubric. This helps us determine the level of evidence. Next, students need to learn to engage themselves in actively reading text because they will read a selected text in order to write an essay in the near future. Readings are selected based on the level of inquiry they will encourage. This begins the process of designing activities to make the desired results happen. By the beginning of week five, students are reading to write.

Collaboration

A teacher's biggest challenge is asking the right questions so students are motivated to inquire. Inquiry-based learning, a form of active learning, aides in the process. It begins with posing questions, problems or scenarios for students to explore. Inquiry-based learning differs from traditional education, where the teacher merely presents facts and his or her knowledge about the subject. Inquiry-based learning is often assisted by a facilitator rather than a lecturer.

Using Inquiry-Based Instruction to build collaboration fosters collective leadership where the teacher is merely the facilitator of the learning. Inquiry-Based Instruction is a unique teaching method that utilizes a student-centered pedagogy to foster deep knowledge and development of lifelong skills by engaging students to become active learners. Inquiry-based Instruction allows for an in-depth investigation related to real life and world problems, provides the environment and the opportunities to explore complex questions and challenges.

Inquiry-Based Instruction moves the student beyond working from an individual point of view to a collaboration setting. Collaborating with peers helps to develop negotiation skills, while working in a group setting and sharing authentic information connected to their lives and experiences. Collaboration leads students into positions of collective leadership by presenting their highest skill level to the group as an expert. Student knowledge can be assessed using Gardner's Theory of Multiple Intelligences and rubrics to illustrate skills the students mastered within the interdisciplinary context. Inquiry-based instruction is a multi-tiered teaching method that provides students with an extended period of time to demonstrate mastery of skills, concepts, understanding and an authentic artifact. Collaborating with colleagues who also teach developmental English reinforces my professional learning community, which keeps me on task and learning new ways to ensure my students learn new skills.

To further develop as an effective educator for my students, I saw a need to feed the senses. Learning feels more engaging when you can touch, hear, smell, and maybe taste a product. Just finishing a project with something you can hold or describe in your own words, because you developed, or made it makes it more tangible and real. Which method to use should not be only one concrete method, but an introduction to a variety of methods based on what the learners need. I developed my ability to look at my students with a holistic approach through communication and assessment.

Inquiry-Based Instruction Scientific Method
Goal: The objective is to Refine, Alter, Expand or Reject the hypotheses.
Step 1 - Make a testable prediction
Step 2 - Collect data
Step 3 - Develop theories/make inferences
Step 4 - Make an observation
Step 5 - Ask relevant questions
Step 6 - Draw conclusion/formulate your hypothesis

Inquiry-Based Instructional Protocol

1. Form Collaborative Peer Teams
   ⇩
2. State a Relative Problem
   ⇩
3. Develop Rubrics for Rules of Engagement
   ⇩
4. Create a Rubric for End Product or Presentation
   ⇩
5. Manage Collaboration
   ⇩
6. Provide Consultation & Feedback
   ⇩
7. Culminate with a Project Celebration

Planning for Inquiry-Based Instruction

A good starting point is to figure out what type of skills, information, results, and or product will illustrate students' mastery in a specific area and how will it add to their real-life experience? Then, the focus needs to address the various methods of assessments to develop a clear understanding of the students' learning styles.

Assessments aid in providing prerequisite skills to ease the transitioning from one skill or academic level to the next. This is necessary for the equity of the experience. Equity means every student in your class has an equal chance and opportunity to learn. Assessments should address the psychological (auditory; visual; tactile) learning. When students participate in a learning environment that fosters holistic instruction, they become engaged, motivated, committed social learners. Teaching considers the procedural aspects related to planning, lesson design, classroom dynamics, instructional techniques and traditional types of assessments. Then take a real look at you and your beliefs, then ask *"Am I flexible enough to give up control and aid the learning process as a facilitator?" "What will it take to make my students/learners successful?" "Will I get support from my peers and administration?"*

Focusing on each type of learner, think about how this project will address the learning needs and skill level, all which will lead to mastery of the subject matter. This leads us to the introspection of yourself and the intersection of our students.

"A teacher is a compass that activates the magnet of curiosity, knowledge, and wisdom in the pupils." Eve Garrison

Rubric Development

In developing a rubric. I consider the skill level mastery for the students to acquire, as well as the components of the project designed for student inquiry. Rubrics then can become a basic guideline for the project and a guideline for the completion and assessment process. These assessment tools are a means to evaluate an end product or performance. There are three types of rubrics:

1. Analytic Rubrics look at the student product with specific criteria of performance which are scored individually. This type provides feedback related to the student's strengths and weaknesses.
2. Developmental Rubrics are a subset of analytic trait rubrics designed to answer the question, "to what extent are students engaged in the programs/services developing this skill/ability/value, etc.?"
3. Holistic Rubrics consists of a single scale with all criteria to be included in the evaluation being considered together based on an overall judgment of the student work. It has an emphasis on what the student is able to demonstrate. Performance Rubrics are the subset. It focuses on tasks or products such as journals, portfolios, and projects and specific skills communication (reading, writing, listening, speaking, psycho-motor and or behavior. Using anchoring points that contribute to the whole, providing a more global use.

When I am developing rubrics, I asked myself the following questions:
- What is the purpose and learning skills of the project?
- What are the objectives or outcome goals? Are the objectives clear?
- Are the expectations/instructions clear?

- What should be included in the criteria list that will be judged (methods of research used, clarity of information and writing, factual accuracy, teamwork and collaboration, visual aesthetics, method of presentation, solution or artifact)
- Did I provide at least three examples that exceeded the basic requirements?
- Assigning four to five columns to describe levels of mastery or proficiency (Beginning/Novice, Developing, Accomplished, Exemplary/Expert) (Emerging, Developing, Meeting. Exceeding).
- Can the students use the rubric to assess their own work for self-improvement?

A well-developed rubric is imperative to Backward Design and Brain-Based Learning. There are four basic elements to a good rubric. They include: Criteria, Levels of Performance, Scores, and Descriptors.

- Criteria: clarifies the meaning of each area of the assignment being assessed. It determines the number of areas of the assignment to be scored.
- Levels of Performance: determines the degree of performance met and tells students what they are expected to do. Sample benchmarks could be as simple as excellent, good, fair, and poor.
- Scores: Students love to see scores and grades. Scores can either encourage or discourage students. Do not forget to include a score for each element and a total score attached to a letter grade.
- Descriptors: also refers to the task of the rubric, describes specifically how the score is derived and describes specifically what work at each level of performance looks. Descriptors determine the degree of performance and the quality of the work.

When all these parts are present, students get a clearer picture of how their work will be assessed and how they earned their grade. I find it more effective when I give students the rubric at the same time I give them the instructions for the assignments. Just as I explain each element of the assignment in detail, I also explain each element of the rubric. This is part of my backward design, helps students get better grades in the end.

Literature – Critical Response Paper Rubric

Total	Descriptor	Not Evident 2 pts	Fairly Evident 4 pts	Emerging 6 pts	Functional 8 pts	Highly Functional 10 pts
	Thesis Statement	There is no thesis statement present at all.	There is a thesis statement present but it is not well developed. It does not have 3 parallel parts and it is not at the end of the introduction.	There is a simple thesis statement present at the end of the introduction. It is not written in 3 parallel parts.	There is a thesis statement at the end of the introduction. There is an attempt to write it in 3 parallel parts but the transition is not functional & part 3 of the thesis is not parallel.	There is a strong, well developed parallel 3 part parallel thesis statement present at the end of the introduction.
	Focus	The subject is ill defined; thesis is not present. There are no original thoughts; Essay has no evidence of being unified. Introduction and/or conclusion is inappropriate. No evidence of a discussion of writer(s) in historical context.	The subject is defined but the thesis is not clear. There are no original thoughts; the essay has little evidence of being unified. The introduction and/or conclusion is ineffective. Vaguely defines writer(s) in historical context.	The subject is fairly well defined; the thesis is fairly clear. There are minimal original thoughts; The essay shows signs of being unified. Fairly developing. Fairly defines writer(s) in historical context.	The subject is well defined; thesis is consistent; The essay has some original thought and is functionally unified with a consistent introduction & conclusion. Clearly defines writer(s) in historical context.	Strong subject; Strong thesis statement; Thoughtful essay with good insight and originality; unified, with effective introduction & conclusion. Strongly defines writer(s) in historical context.
	Organization	No evidence of a plan; even opinions are stated without a logical order; many digressions and gaps exists	A plan was attempted but is difficult to infer; the thesis is present but not written in 3 clear parts, points are neither logical nor signaled by transitions; some digressions and some gaps exists.	There is a noticeable plan and thesis at the end of the introduction but perhaps unclear or incomplete; some major points are signaled by transitions; most points are logical and related; but a few digressions and gaps exists.	The plan is clear; clear thesis at the end of the introduction; most major points are signaled by commonplace transitions at begin other paragraphs; some minor digressions or gaps exist.	A plan is evident and major points are signaled by strong thesis at the end of the introduction & appropriate transitions to begin other paragraphs; neither digressions nor gaps exist.
	Development	The thesis is abstract with few or no specifics; only vague & general ideas are expressed with little to	The thesis is poorly explained with frequent unsupported generalizations and/or redundant expressions or ideas;	The thesis is fairly well explained and developed in 5 paragraphs; there are some unsupported generalizations or	Adequate thesis; explained and fairly well developed in an adequate 5 paragraph essay with adequate	Strong & well developed thesis into a 5 paragraph essay with a strong intro, body, with strong details, examples & conclusion

Literature – Critical Response Paper Rubric

		no real focus. No discussion of literary devices used in the writing.	persons some irrelevant details exists. Vague discussion of literary devices used in the writing	irrelevant details present. Developing discussion of literary devices used in the writing.	details and specific examples. Functional discussion of literary devices used in the writing.	w/no new discussion devices us writing.
	Vocabulary & Word Choice	Very limited use of vocabulary, irrappropriate word choices; and unclear & confusing meanings.	Vague, a bit confusing at times, inappropriate word choice, cliché, colloquial, or informal language exists.	Some clear, appropriate word choice, but at times the oversimplified; and faulty idiom(s) exists.	Clear language, usually appropriate word choice; perhaps some use of figurative language.	Precise & word cho even a go figurative
	Syntax (Sentence Structure)	High frequency of errors, preventing clear understanding of the content of the essay. Very difficult to read.	Tangled and unclear syntax; frequent uncertain sentence boundaries; occasional range of syntactical choices. A little difficult to read.	Generally appropriate expressions but some major errors exist; but overall command of basic sentence structure; narrow arrange range of syntactical choices.	Good control of syntax, with occasional errors in some complex sentences; reading the essay is not very difficult.	Strong syntax, use o sentence ea
	Mechanics (Grammar, Spelling, and Punctuation)	Numerous and major errors, especially agreement errors; ignored basic writing conventions.	Frequent errors in grammar, spelling, and punctuation; some agreement errors exists; little understanding of basic writing conventions.	Usually correct grammar, spelling, & punctuation; shows slight understanding of basic writing conventions; evidence of slight proofreading exists.	With few exceptions, correct grammar, spelling, & punctuation; shows some evidence proofreading and shows some understanding of writing conventions.	Strong us grammar, punctuati use of wr conventic easy to re Proofrea evident
	Response to Reading	Demonstrates poor understanding of the reading. No evidence of information and/or key points from reading selection; quoting is incorrectly cited or unrelated to claims.	Demonstrates limited understanding of key points of the reading; summaries, paraphrasing, and quoting is limited and hardly related to claims.	Demonstrates accurate but limited understanding of key points of the reading; makes some relevant references; inaccurate or omitted summaries; paraphrasing and quoted to support claims.	Demonstrates generally accurate understanding of key points of the reading; references; uses some summaries, paraphrasing, and quotations to support claims.	Demonst understa points o make referenc summarie and quotal c
	MLA Style	Ignored MLA style.	Vague use	Developing use	Functional use	Highly f

Nothing beats a failure but a try!

Once during my science class, I noticed two students continue to struggle with their project's formative assessment. One student had excellent notes and reflections that were in chronological order by date. However, he was unsuccessful in transferring the information to the assessment. The second student had no notes but she qualifies her project progress in a one-to-one session. So, I paired the students together with a goal to develop a method of note-taking and transference that worked for both of them. Well, the note taker explained his reflections and notes to the other student who turned out to be an amazing artist. She drew what the first student explained to her. As they worked together they learned how to take notes so they could remember and understand the content as well as transfer the information from the reflections to the formative assessment.

I make sure I talk to the learners! I ask what is the "BIG QUESTION" or "REAL-LIFE ISSUE" they would like to work on. In this questioning session, I explain completing the project will be challenging yet important work! Phil Schlechty (1994) explained students who are engaged exhibit three characteristics. When I take the necessary steps described by Schlechty, I see these characteristics in my students more often than not.

1. They are attracted to their work.
2. They persist in their work despite challenges and obstacles,
3. They visibly delight in accomplishing their work.

Next is "Brainstorming Objectives", the results of the group discussion to solve a problem or produce a product. During the brainstorming sessions, the instructor and the students must develop some basic rules. As an educator, my expectations are to:
- Be Respectful
- Allow the person speaking to complete their thoughts
- To accept no idea as a bad idea
- Take risks
- Be creative
- No criticism allowed

The activity should have a note-taker, timekeeper and a small group of no more than 4-5 students. Keep it short, 10 to 15 minutes. Each group should then review ideas, have a speaker and summarize their top 6-10 ideas. The next step then is the selection of the topic/issue/focus. Research the idea and generate the actions to turn ideas into reality.

Stay committed to your decision but stay flexible in your approach.

Encompassing a myriad of set goals and outcomes with a variety of activities will give students a springboard to initiate and promote their own learning with facilitated support. Students will become abreast of working in small groups, independent research, and leading presentations. Inquiry-based learning helps to build trust between students and teachers with the development of an interpersonal relationship that provides a positive and stimulating environment, where learning can take place. In providing a safe student-conducted, open communication environment, it will increase student-to-student verbal and physical interaction.

As I learned to develop, implement, and assess project-based learning with class lessons, students became more comfortable and confident with discussions and with the development with their personal academic skills which they could now better illustrate by the completion of the project. My students usually become motivated and maintain a high positive attitude as their projects progressed. It was difficult at first because they were accustomed to working one on one as opposed to working in a group setting. They were not accustomed to the concept of questioning and defending their own research and processes. Students who would not normally volunteer to respond to questions developed self-confidence and were eventually successful in defending their research and processes. To assist in the process, I rearranged the desks to semi-circle or circle set up to encourage collaboration and community.

Time

Time is one of the most critical components of a successful project. Projects must have efficient time to plan, time to change when and if there is a need due to an issue or situation. There needs to be time to complete the project, and time to give the presentations and a culminating activity. Also, there needs to be time for the instructor to critique the work, determine conceptual clarity of the focus of the project, and presenting options and possibilities of additional topics.

High-quality inquiry projects demonstrate and reinforce a variety of skills that enhances their college readiness, technology research, and workforce training that's inclusive for our special needs students and our gifted students with the purpose to advance all of our student's skills. The results are students who are globally connected with self-actualization of universal collective needs and desire and direction to obtain feed forward goals, as educators, we understand that we are developing students of all ages to have the following dispositions:

- The ability to recognize and evaluate their own strength.
- The ability to evaluate their own learning style(s).
- Reflect on their growth.
- Effectively communicate through oral and written languages and the arts.
- Display independence in applying a variety of learning strategies and use of resources to accomplish a task.
- Be environmentally, socially, and ethically responsible members of the community.
- Be responsible for self, property, and classroom duties.
- Respect the culture and diversity of others.
- Use appropriate social skills to accomplish a goal with others.
- Have the basic skills to support learning and the accomplishment of higher-level tasks.
- Be independent thinkers who respond critically to a variety of materials and perspectives offered through diverse media.
- Make learning internal and reflective.

Implementation of Inquiry-Based Projects

As discussed in chapter 2, Inquiry-Based Learning is best implemented in a blended learning environment. The facilitating instructor grows as a resourceful, quick-witted, and creative. Yet the facilitating instructor understands how to design and plan excellent learning experiences for students that are aligned to state standards or SLO's. They grow in building a culture of inquiry, personalize preparation, and scaffolding skills. Though the facilitating instructor expects students to manage the steps in a project, they assess students' work regularly to ensure the final product will be the highest quality and students are successful. The facilitating instructor keeps the driving question in mind and allows for flexibility, while also keeping track of the details, during the learning process.

Before the project
As you think about your project design, decide what you want to happen and the product and deliverable you anticipate. Decide the student learning outcomes you expect. Plan for deep and active learning with no regard for perfection. Be a friend of change, be open to adjusting when necessary. Be open to learning about learning. Create a checklist for your project and then design a rubric detailing your expectations. Be sure to include all parts of the rubric development. See chapter 2.

During the project
Decide what students need to know before they start the project, and decide what they may need to read. Analyze data, identify and clarify misconceptions. Get a feel for the possibilities for selected topics within the inquiry. Monitor their activity during the implementation of the project, and ask probing questions that promote deeper learning. Guide them to the information needed to finish the project. Dig into big ideas, relevant inquiries, and engaging questions. Help students raise more questions to ensure the direction of the project.

After the project
You will need to facilitate the completion of the product and deliverables. You may need to help students outline a project that combines interests and standards. Your role as facilitator is project development, implementation, monitoring, and directing the progression of the project while adjusting if necessary. Guide students through the design of manageable and logical solutions to address problems posed before and during the project.

Sample Inquiry-based humanities, literature and, and social science project ideas

"Creativity is especially expressed in the ability to make connections, to make associations, to turn things around and express them in a new way." Tim Hansen

1. **Most inquiry-based learning project begins with questions such as:**
   - What do you want to know?
   - What do you know?
   - What are your career goals?
   - What are the controversial issues you identify in your career path?
   - How can we be the change we want to see in the world?
   - Locate a social issue of personal concern that affects our world.

   Students will be able to:

   - Write a research paper using reliable sources of information.
   - Implement an information gathering action plan related to their chosen topic.
   - Share their learning at a team-wide exhibition.

   Product & Deliverables:

   - Research paper with an annotated bibliography and literature review.
   - IMovie, video blog, written blog, podcast, website, or Scrapbook (to document action plan)
   - Booth at Exhibition (e.g., pamphlets and information to share with the public)

2. **WHAT is in a WORD?**

Link the project to a historian, a specific author, a specific era, or a specific piece of literature.

As a nation, there is a need to reflect on the choice of words used by others to describe another ethnic group or a person who is different. Words used by one group toward another group or person can be viewed as inflammatory, bias, stereotypical or blatantly racist. In either case, it is insensitive to an individual or group alike. Whether in a personal, social or professional setting, we must become more aware and conscientious of the words we are projecting into the hearts and minds of people specifically and society in general. We must be clear that words have the power to shape our characters as well as to define our reality. Let us engage in creating a beautiful and harmonious reality for each other and ourselves. This journey is to examine our world and ourselves as we explore "What is in a Word?"

Introduction
   Part 1: Historically many words have been used in unflattering, negative and destructive ways because, overall, people have lost or never understood the power of words to create and destroy characters, families, and societies. Each student will select a set of words (minimum of two words) to illustrate their historical, societal effect. Partner with two other students with

words related to creating an event or conflict. Each project must include the following information:
1. Historical Outlook-descriptively expresses the mood of the country.
2. Create a timeline (50-year time span) related to the specific word.
3. Create and conduct a survey (asking at least 2 people ages 17- 30 or 31-80) with at least 10 questions related to the group.
4. Write a 2-page paper comparing and contrasting the historical and current use of the word.
5. Write a 1-page: Research and document the cultural influences of the use of the word and how the word in each cultural group and where the word is used to influence the way the English languages are spoken.
6. List and describe any written or spoken research related to the word(s).
7. Listen to a musical selection that promotes a positive image or negative image and explain the image in detail including how and why (1 page).
8. Locate and cite how the words are used in movies or books (name the movie or book).
   - What will be your criteria for the project?
   - What will you need to provide for the students?
   - Will you create or need a rubric?
   - What type of presentation will be required?
   - What is the timeline?

3. **Then and Now-Now and What?**

Introduction

Inventions and scientific discoveries are constantly changing how we live. They cause a new way. Faster, or easier. Increasing production, productivity, and or saving a life or curing an illness. Where would we be without them?

Students will research an invention or scientific discovery that describes the time period, a current event of that time (then).

- What was happening before the discovery or invention? What did it look like?
- How did the discovery or invention happen/ why did it happen?
- Now-how has the discovery/invention to improve life? What does it look like now?
- What will it do and how will it improve lives? What will it look like in the future?
- Illustration must show past, present, and future.

4. Societal Stereotypes

Introduction

The children's poem, "Sticks and stones will break my bones, but words will never hurt me" is not a true statement. It is the biggest lie ever told to our children. It has a historical lack of accountability. It actually encourages bullying and societal stereotypes instead of changing them. Societal stereotypes cause others to be labeled, bullied, discriminated against, taunted, bruised, insulted, criticized, ridiculed, mocked, and goaded. These unflattering, negative, and unvarying degrees of ill-treatment which children and various ethnic groups experience because of their apparent differences are detrimental.

This project was created to provide a platform of understanding leading to tolerance, acceptance, and pride. Historically, many ethnic groups have been treated negatively because others have delivered a fixed negative idea about their specific community.

Part 1 *"Stereotypes do exist, but we have to walk through them." Forest Whitaker*

This portion of the school-wide project will allow each student to select an ethnic group to illustrate their historical societal stereotypes. Each project must include the following information:
- Historical outlook - descriptively express the mood of the country.
- Create a timeline (50-year time span) related to the specific group.
- Create and conduct a survey (asking 50 people (the number could change based on the grade level of the students creating the project) age 8-13, 14-30 or 31-80 with at least 10 questions related to the group. Your questions must be approved before you conduct your survey. You must also complete the workshop on a Likert Scale.
- Identify someone within the group you selected to interview. You must tell the instructor why you chose that person and what you think you can learn from him or her. You must also get your questions approved by the instructor before conducting the interview.
- Write a 5-paragraph paper comparing and contrasting of choice to another ethnic group.
- Research and document the cultural influences of their dialect and how they may include these influences in the way they speak the English language.
- List and describe any scientific or medical research related to the group.
- Why is image important?

Part 2 "Image is everything" or so they say!
Answer the following questions about the ethnic group of your choice.
1. What does your image say to others? Include the following: the style of dress, mannerisms, hairstyle, dialect, and vocabulary, etc.
2. Evaluate a sitcom or movie and explain what image is being displayed?

3. Observe at least two of your peers, identify and explain how their image promotes a positive image. Without mentioning names, select 1 person in the same age group in any visual medium whose image promotes a negative image. Explain why?
4. Analyze a music video that promotes a positive image and explain the image in detail. Include how and why?
5. Analyze a music video that promotes a negative image and explain the image in detail. Include how and why?
6. Compare and contrast contemporary positive images and stereotypes around you.
7. Arrange the information gathered and formulate them into a 3-5-minute video or 2-minute commercial of your findings.

5. Investigate the journey of food from growth to consumption, then to disposal

Driving questions
- How do foods affect our minds and bodies?
- How do we decide on the foods we eat?
- Where do foods come from?
- How does food make it to our plates?
- What are the effects of the resources that go into the whole process of food consumption?
- How is food regulated in your state?
- How is it regulated by the country?

Part 1 Food systems

Students will
- Learn how food grows
- Explore how it is manufactured, packaged it, and shipped
- Discover how to buy it and sell it
- Trace political and economic impacts of food choices

Part 1 Health & Wellness

Students will...
- Study how food is consumed and disposed of
- Learn what our bodies need in order to grow and function
- Explore the effects of certain types of food on them

Products and deliverables
- Produce a commercial for some of the foods you are learning about
- Map the lifecycle of a specific food product from start to finish
- Producing a full-length documentary on Food Systems and the Human Food Chain

- Develop a food product for sale and any other digital branding and media for your product.

6. Music and its effects on society

Essential questions
- What is the media? Is music part of the media?
- What influences music?
- Does music influence the behavior of children? Teens? Adults?
- Where did the love go in today's black pop music?
- Why are genuine love songs harder to find?
- How has the rise of rap changed perceptions of love?
- What has the influence of streaming on the Billboard charts done for music about love?
- Have perceptions of love played a part in music? If so, how? If not, why?

The student will
- Engage in a discussion about what transitions in music, and bring in examples.
- Explore how music changes in lyrics in R & B music lyrics have transitioned.
- Trace and map the change in R & B music and develop a timeline of changes from 1979-1999; OR
- Trace and map changes in R & B music and develop a timeline of changes from 2000-2020.
- Analyze lyrics in R & B music related to the timeline selected using charts and graphs.

Products & Deliverables
- Write an essay discussing your findings. (I usually require an essay and another deliverable brings the research to life.)
- Produce a commercial for some of the foods you are learning about
- Map the lifecycle of a specific food product from start to finish
- Producing a full-length documentary on Food Systems and the Human Food Chain
- Develop a food product for sale and any other digital branding and media for your product.
- Research paper with an annotated bibliography and literature review.
- IMovie, video blog, written blog, podcast, website, or Scrapbook (to document action plan)
- Booth at Exhibition (e.g., pamphlets and information to share with the public)

Scholar's Circle Literary Project Video

Assignment Instructions

1. Choose a group of 3-5 peers

2. Decide the theme for your video.
    - Which era? (Civil Rights, Black Arts Movement, or Harlem Renaissance)
    - What was the social climate?
    - What critical thinking questions does the era spark in readers?

3. Evaluate 3 writers,
    - Their background and works
    - Literary devices used by the writers
    - What critical thinking questions does the writers spark in readers?

4. Write a script for a 3-5-minute video
5. Record your video for an in-class film screening
6. Consult the categories in the assignment rubric to ensure you are following all instructions.

To ensure your Midterm Literary Project has an action plan and follows it so your project is completed on time, eac[h] should be assigned a role. Should your group consist of 4 members, the 4th member will act as an assistant to both t[he] supervisor and the videographer.

Facilitator - This student is tasked to monitor and assist the work of all other group members. The facilitator is in c[harge of] organizing the final product of the project, be it a paper, a presentation, etc. That doesn't mean technical details, but that the project meets the standards set out by the instructor (often as a rubric), plus any extras stipulated by the grou[p.] Standards generally include punctuality and completeness. This student gets discussion, action plan, and production it moving, often by asking the other group members questions, sometimes about what they've just been saying or do[ing to move the] project forward. The facilitator supervises practice sessions in preparation for recording and works with the script s[upervisor and the] videographer to deciding upon. The Facilitator secures a location for recording day. Should the group consist of 4 [members, the] facilitator will ensure the 4th person is active in his or her role as assistant to the script supervisor and the videograp[her.]

Script Supervisor – The script project gathers story ideas from other members and puts it together. This person tak[es] the group meets and keeps track of group data/sources/etc. This person distributes these notes to the rest of the grou[p and] sections relevant for their parts of the project. This student will listen to what others say and explain it back in his o[r her own words,] asking the original speaker if the interpretation is correct and ensure others' ideas an appropriately used in the script[.] [The script] supervisor is responsible for preparing the script for video recording day.

Videographer - This student would be responsible for the technical details of the product. The student is responsib[le for] production and works directly with the script supervisor to set the stage for recording day. The videographer will re[...]

Scholar's Circle Literary Project Video

Professor Yisrael   African American Literature 121

Which Era? _____   Which 3 Authors? _____

Student's Names: _____

CATEGORY	5 points	4 points	3 points	1 points
Preparedness	The video shows preparedness and the group has obviously rehearsed and created the video as a fluid group exemplarily.	The video shows preparedness and the group has obviously rehearsed and created the video as a fluid group effectively.	The video shows preparedness and the group has obviously rehearsed and created the video as a fluid group acceptably.	The group does not seem prepared to record the video at all.
Content	Shows an exemplary understanding of the author and his or her writing.	Shows an effective understanding of the topic author and his or her writing.	Shows an acceptable understanding of the topic author and his or her writing.	Shows a developing understanding of the topic author and his or her writing.
Collaboration with Peers	Demonstrates an exemplary and collaborative effort among Scholars Circle Group members.	Demonstrates an effective collaborative effort among Scholars Circle Group members.	Demonstrates an acceptable collaborative effort among Scholars Circle Group members.	Demonstrates a developing collaborative effort among Scholars Circle Group members.
Critical Thinking Questions	Indicates an exemplary understanding of critical thinking questions	Indicates an effective understanding of critical thinking questions	Indicates an acceptable understanding of critical thinking questions	Indicates a developing understanding of critical thinking questions

Evaluation of the Author's writing	The evaluation of the author's piece of writing was exemplary.	The evaluation of the author's piece of writing was effective.	The evaluation of the author's piece of writing was acceptable.	The evaluation of the author's piece of writing was developing.
Author's Life & Purpose	The group included interesting information about the author's life and purpose for his or her writing in an exemplary manner.	The group included interesting information about the author's life and purpose for his or her writing in an effective manner.	The group included interesting information about the author's life and purpose for his or her writing in an acceptable manner.	The group did not include interesting information about the author's life and purpose for his or her writing.
Social Climate of the Era in History	The group included exemplary information about the era and the social climate that existed from the text	The group included effective information about the era and the social climate that existed from the text.	The group included acceptable information about the era and the social climate that existed from the text	The group included very little to no information about the era and the social climate that existed from the text.
Other Research	The group included other research about the author and his or her writing in an exemplary manner.	The group included other research about the author and his or her writing in an effective manner.	The group included other research about the author and his or her writing in an acceptable manner.	Other research was hardly evident or did not exist at all.
Presentation Creativity	The video has music, color, art, and voice over and uses it creatively in an exemplary way.	The video has music, color, art, and voice over and uses it creatively and effectively.	The video has music, color, art, and voice over and the creativity is acceptable.	The creativity of the presentation was hardly existed. There is no music, color, art, or voice over.

3
Restorative Practices

Restorative practices helped students to recover from the abuse they experienced in other academic settings and helped them learn to entrust in education again. When I think about current educational environments with its "quick-to-fix-the-problem" response to daily challenges, it is clear our reactionary quickness has only exacerbated the problems facing educational reform. One must hold a consistent moral position and act explicitly from moral principles on given issues while at the same time not succumbing to the dead-end closure of judgmentalism (Fullan, 2008). This means we have to view each situation that demands attention with detachment. We can't get caught up in the melodramatics of what's happening with any given situation without first realizing there is a "situation."

Too many times in the past we react too quickly without understanding the full scope of all that we see. When this happens, we fail the student by giving them control of things when it's our responsibility to be chief communicators and leaders resolving all conflict or without using that 'cookie-cutter' resolve. For example, a student comes to class unable to function because of issues from home. Without prior knowledge or a relational connection to this student as the 'whole child,' the teacher will have no clue of what's motivating his actions. As a result, the teacher may be quick to reprimand the student, which only intensifies an adverse outcome.

Restorative justice intends to determine strategies to quell confrontations and problems by focusing on transformational solutions that address accountability, ownership and collaboration of all vested participants (Wachtel, T., n.d.). The use of restorative practices helps to reduce crimes, violence, bullying, and in this case, can build 'affective' relationships between teacher and student. These practices provide effective leadership as well as it repairs the harm done. As a teacher with transformational, situational, and servant leadership skills, he or she is in a better position for building stronger relationships with effective channels of communication.

To underscore a need to know the student; what each students' needs and triggers are; to tailor a plan of action that best serves each student is essential in relationship building. Restorative practices encompass the 'whole' child concept in that it differentiates the needs of each child so a tailor-made plan of action to decided and implemented. With restorative practices as the sentinels for keeping a balance between teacher/student perceptions and behaviors, we perhaps stand a better chance for relevant reformation and systemic change. To do so will require educational leaders in the classroom to become effective communicators and constructivists in relationship-building.

With the usage of restorative practices, teachers, as transformational, situational and servant leaders, and active listeners, harness the capacity to end possible conflicts. They understand the personal needs of the students and are relentless in attending to them. This leadership style persuades the student to engage and participate in clearing up problems. Restorative practices bring humanity back to the table. When exercised with the wellbeing of the child in mind, jurisprudence no longer becomes the major factor in decision making. Today's children's concerns are compounded by deeper issues than just lawful infractions. History has borne witness to many black and brown children incarcerated for lesser crimes than their white counterparts due to demographics and ethnicity. For the same crime, a non-colored child will be given community service or probation, whereas, that child of color may be given unwarranted penal time. Humanity must drive decision-making, not only in the classroom but throughout society. Restorative practices are guided by tolerance, humaneness, clemency, and generosity.

Education had become so completely complicated that by the time our students were 15 or 16, it was a common phenomenon for those who began our program before age 4 to read, write and think beyond the 12th-grade level. Our students were engaged in project-based learning before project-based learning had a name. We provided a variety of novels and reading which sparked a joy for learning. We encourage our children to dream and dream big. We encouraged them to look ahead and have a dream for their lives and academic plan that would help to ensure they fulfilled those dreams and reached those goals. We would often have to find internships for these students to explore career options, targeting the program they would study in college. And, yes, not enrolling in college was not an option.

When our high school students took the ACT tests they typically scored off the charts. This was not because they were so smart but because they could think and they could read a variety of complex text, and they could persevere, they learned to have a growth mindset, they learned to have grit. We encouraged them to feel comfortable with making mistakes, learn from them, and learn to fix them or do things another way to get different or better results. Unfortunately, when students enrolled in our school after 4th- 6th grade, usually, they did not make these types of educational gains and making mistakes scares them. The sooner we get them, the better.

When I was principal at an alternative high school on the southside of Chicago, I used music as the cue to change classes instead of a bell. We opened the school day with a large restorative justice peace circle so students could check-in and get their minds ready for class. I always begin teaching the students in front of me the same way, establishing expectations, setting them up for success, getting to know them as students, and developing professional relationships. Because the alternative high school students were generally far behind in high school credit when they enrolled, we created ½ credit research projects they could complete and earn extra credit. Teachers created cross-curricular projects that were relevant to urban life to engage students and get them excited about learning. Our goal was to recapture the excitement they lost in the primary grades. This is usually the time students start to have difficulty in school and lag behind.

I have taught at City Colleges of Chicago's Kennedy-King campus for 12 years, 7 years as full-time faculty and 5 years as an adjunct. What I have learned is that academic levels do not matter. Students who are academically dysfunctional suffer from the same things. They are deficient of skill, unmotivated, lack passion for learning, and am currently in a position hearts have rarely been touched by a teacher. Aristotle stated, "Educating the mind without educating the heart is no education at all." I attempt to pattern my instructional practices in this way. Active learning has been a part of my background and my experience in urban education.

Currently, I teach African American literature, composition, and developmental courses at a community college on the south side of Chicago. I am a tenure assistance program mentor for new faculty and faculty development coordinator for the campus teaching and learning center. I am constantly reflecting on my role as a facilitator of learning for the students I teach as well as the faculty I coordinate and mentor. I am dreaming of a perfect classroom environment with perfect students who are happy and eager and more than willing to sit still and quiet and ready to listen to me talk. My hope is for them to write everything down with eagerness, and understand every idea, agree with it without question, and regurgitate it on a test so I can prove to my superiors that I am a teacher! Though I know it does not exist, a person can dream, can't she!

The restorative justice process is facilitated by a teacher or mediator with no judgment. The person needing the mediation, the student who caused the harm and the person who was harmed is in a circle to address the problem. The mediator asked the questions, "What happened? How did it happen? What can we do to make it right?" Relationships grow stronger through the use of discussion in the restorative justice process. It is about building relationships and repairing harm. However, restorative practice is a strategy whereby teachers use a preventive approach BEFORE harm is done. The E.N.G.A.G.E. classroom management approach is a restorative practice that includes the healing of intrapersonal intelligence, effective communication, and collaboration that fosters collective leadership, and well planning for student achievement, thereby, making every minute count, which allows teachers to manage students with ease.

Rarely do students enrolled in at-risk urban schools consider themselves strong or smart. They are more than likely not being encouraged to be lifelong learners and rarely taught about growth in mindset. Many secondary or post-secondary students from urban schools have not been taught to have a strong academic work ethic and may not have the tools necessary to propel themselves forward in either their academic or personal lives. Consequently, many are academically abused as they are passed from grade to grade without appropriate skill levels to do well in the next grade level. Some give up on school and choose to go to work at menial jobs providing them with a poor quality of life. However, some have not given up on their educational pursuits and occupational dreams and seek a more intensive educational approach in order to grasp the core concepts needed to successfully complete college and/or vocational programs. Young people are supposed to desire more in foundational years.

By the time a child gets to high school they should be able to write a decent multi-paragraph summative or expository essay. They should know that they have an opinion and be able to support their opinions, at least basically. High school is where they learn to elaborate on their opinions, conduct basic research, and cite the sources they use. They should not be afraid of all thing's academics; they should not fear reading; they should not be stressed by writing; they should love to learn, yet so many high school students have a disdain for learning; no adult took time to help them identify their talents and get passionate about it. Everything colleges teach in remedial, foundational, or developmental education courses should be skills students learned before high school. Unfortunately, though many urban high schools are given students with little to no literacy skills, skills targeted in third-sixth grades. These are the levels that need a complete revamping.

Urban students are students who often struggle academically during their first and second years of college. They usually need tutoring, individual time with the instructor, and mentoring in some cases. These are students who may have either been underprepared or ill-prepared for the postsecondary education classroom. They may have been beaten down by others in their academic path and frightened by a lack of or limited success. Restorative practice has not been part of their academic experience. Thus, they drop out due to poor motivation and lack of university ready skills. Within the past decade not only has the high school dropout rates increased, but young people are also dropping out of upper elementary school in droves. Our youth experience negative employment and negative life outcomes far too early. Educators know that poverty often leads to incarceration as well as very poor mental and physical health. Instructors who teach foundational studies and developmental education college students have multifaceted responsibilities.

This is my experience as an urban educator and community college instructor. We need to address student's issues of cognition as well as the affective domain. The affective domain is the part of educational psychologist Dr. Benjamin Bloom's work higher education teachers want to ignore, partly because we are not sure about the specific behavior for which we should expect or look for. It requires us to understand, reflect upon, and design our courses with values, stereotypes, feelings, and attitudes under consideration. The affective domain also includes motivation or lack of motivation as well as what motivates a student. Educators tend to put our focus on the cognitive domain, rarely do we attempt to educate the whole child or the whole student in college settings. We want students to know, understand, comprehend, analyze, evaluate, and synthesize, while not giving the affective domain enough attention. It is easier to identify the behavior we should expect or look for in the cognitive domain; ultimately, these are the behaviors we use to apply grades. It is the goal of E.N.G.A.G.E. classroom planning approach to address issues of the affective domain. This is my personal focus at the beginning of the courses I teach so that I am better able to work with students in the cognitive domain.

The focus of the E.N.G.A.G.E. approach is to empower teachers to give students the necessary tools that will allow them to have self-control, be cooperative and responsible during our course and beyond. As a community college instructor, I believe the adults I teach come to class with experiential knowledge and that they too have the ability to share valuable information during the course. However, I am cautious about maintaining a distinct understanding of our teacher/student relationship. As the authority in the course, I make it clear that the knowledge I am teaching is the primary focus and priority. I am open and firm in communicating course expectations for comportment. I would be doing my students a grave injustice if I were too laissez-faire in my approach that they do not reach the expected outcomes.

I try to be consistent with my classroom management approach while at the same time structuring each class so that student learning outcomes are reached. I never allow "feelings" to take precedence over classroom control. Student feelings are not allowed to dictate the trajectory of the class. Daily class objectives are set, and I strive to ensure these objectives are met using a balanced approach that allows for mutual respect and appreciation.

I am not the autocratic instructor who believes an authoritarian approach is what is necessary to control students. I believe the adults I teach come to class with experiential learning and knowledge, I am not the sole knower in the classroom. Though I do not try to be a "friend", I am open and firm in communicating course expectations for appropriate academic comportment. I am open to verbal interaction but I am not seeking to be the "cool" teacher with a democratic approach. There are set student learning outcomes for the course and I would be doing my students a grave injustice if I were too cavalier in my approach that they do not reach the expected outcomes. I try to be consistent with my classroom management approach while at the same time structuring each class so that student learning outcomes are reached. I never allow "feelings" to take precedence over classroom control. Student feelings are not allowed to dictate the trajectory of the class. Daily class objectives are set, and I strive to ensure these objectives are met without being neither authoritative nor a laissez-faire instructor.

Thus, I am a reflective teacher and have created a self-review process. I look at what needs to be done in each class session in order to reach student learning outcomes think about what I need to do in order for students to do what they need to do. I reflect upon what has worked in prior semesters and what did not work. Further, I identify and explore my own instructional beliefs and practices. This almost always leads to changes and improvements in my teaching, sometimes even an entire transformation. For me, classroom management is all about improving my teaching techniques. When I teach, student comportment is engaging and they are deeply involved in the coursework. When this happens, there may be noise in the classroom, but it is organized noise. Students are engaging with each other, asking questions and giving feedback in Scholars Circle groups and I am circulating the room also asking questions, answering questions, and giving feedback.

      I use formative assessments to monitor my teaching and try to clearly stated expectations and model them. I am open to reintroducing concepts based on formative assessments either to individual students or the entire class as a whole. I study the characteristics of an adult learner and try to utilize these characteristics to set students up for success, not failure. I respect the learners who sit in front of me as the adults they are and I am prepared to learn from them as well. This E.N/G.A.G.E. approach to active learning was designed to empower those who work with our youth to empower students to desire to learn, to help them enjoy learning, and to place them on the path of being a lifelong learner. This will be the key to the success of urban students.

How I Prepare to Teach

     The goal for the current courses I teach at the community college level is to give students a crash course in literacy and college preparedness. In many cases, my students have little to no college preparedness compounded by tremendous and sometimes overwhelming personal challenges and social struggles. Such challenges and struggles often result in disruptive and uncooperative behavior. I try to take the affective domain of Bloom's Taxonomy, student motivation, attitudes, perceptions, and values into consideration as I plan. I know their learning can either be inhibited or enhanced if not. The whole student concept is not simply the cognitive domain, which includes remembering, comprehending, analyzing, evaluating, and creating. The affective domain, usually ignored by educators, is also imperative for teaching the whole-child, the whole-student. This classroom reality makes course preparation imperative with the syllabus being the primary and most vital component. Course preparation is the foundation for a progressive and productive semester. Teaching developmental courses requires that I devise and implement many strategies to inspire and encourage cooperative learning. The implementation of such strategies is not possible without my attention to many course preparation details.

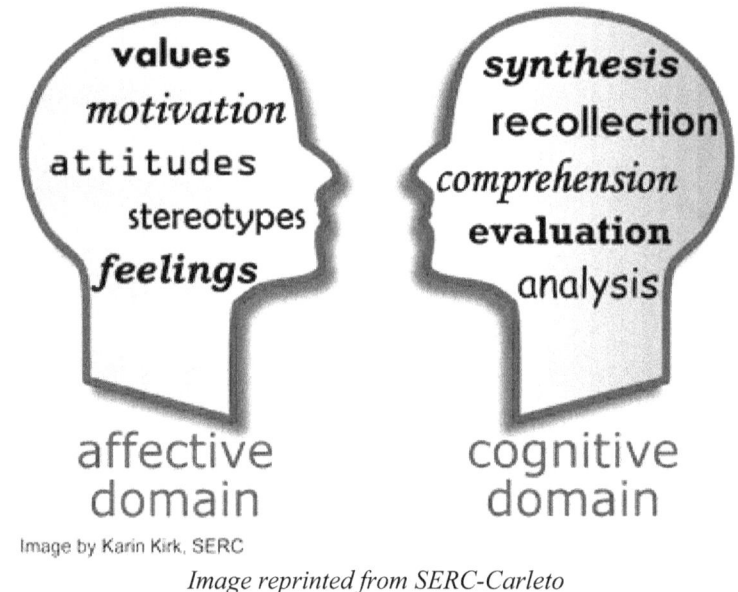

Image reprinted from SERC-Carleto
- Carleton College

     I help students improve their academic skills so that they can successfully complete college-level coursework and eventually graduate. Often students do not feel good about having to take developmental courses and this is why my presentation and delivery must be carefully tailored to ensure that the self-esteem and confidence of my students are built up and encouraged. Further, I create strategies that allow me to observe, notate and address specific signs of disruptive behavior or challenges with comprehension and assignment completion.

     My presentation and delivery are geared to ensure that I meet the needs of my students. Due to my student's personal and social challenges, I know that they need to feel a sense of mutual respect. I have to exhibit that I am understanding and compassionate so that they will feel comfortable approaching me to ask questions, share their personal problems and seek advice. I have to establish my role as the authority in what I am teaching in a way where their dignity remains intact and their pride is upheld. My students need to experience an intellectually engaging environment that is not overwhelming, stressful or too difficult to participate in. Further, they need the opportunity to engage in meaningful activities that instill within them a permanent understanding of the lessons taught in the course to prepare them for college-level coursework.

Experience has allowed me to understand how critical course preparation and syllabus delivery truly is within developmental education. If I neglect to properly prepare and set the stage during the first two classes, more than likely, the following classes will be very difficult to manage and many students will be uncooperative and unruly. My approach to classroom management is relationship building, and again it begins with my syllabus. My first responsibility is to create a meaningful connection between myself, students and the subject matter. I found that if I do not focus my attention on linking these three components of teaching and learning for my students from the onset, then we may certainly experience challenges throughout the remainder of the course.

I believe students have difficulty learning from instructors who they do not respect, appreciate or like. I've heard many instructors say to students, "I'm here to teach not to be liked." This is not my philosophy. Actually, being likable allows for my delivery of course material to be palatable and comprehensible. I take great care to prevent the arising of negative emotions that can cause students to shut down, become defensive and reactionary within the classroom setting. In preparation for my current courses I complete the following tasks:

1. Re-evaluate the student learning outcomes for the course.
2. Examine the course textbook to see if it has been changed by the department.
3. Determine if I need to supplement with additional educational materials.
4. Examine the course's topical outline and decide if it needs to be altered and updated
5. Align the course outline with the current calendar.
6. Review, adjust and update the policies and procedures listed in the syllabus.
7. Review and update all PowerPoint Presentations developed for the course.
8. Review and update the required reading book list of novels for the course
9. Read every current novel added to the book list.
10. Design study questions, group assignments, and essay topics for the novels added to the book list.
11. Review literary devices and decide how the author uses them in the novel.
12. Research new strategies for teaching writing in higher education.
13. Read, study, and attend webinars, workshops and/or conferences, to discover new and improved techniques and strategies for teaching writing.
14. Communicate with colleagues, who also teach writing, and learn about their discoveries, effective teaching strategies, and techniques.
15. Review the Course Management webpage developed for my previous course.
16. Create a Course Management web page for the upcoming course.
17. Draft an encouraging welcome message, briefly outlining course expectations and post on the course's Blackboard announcement section.

Course preparedness is essential for the completion of a successful course with a high passing rate. Such preparedness is even more essential for college-level developmental education courses. I am passionate about equipping my students with the rudiments of writing required to complete college-level course assignments of every subject and gain more writing skills with more advanced writing courses.

The purpose of my role in the E.N.G.A.G.E. approach is to share my experience with educators regarding preparing young people in front of us for the next level. We build an academic foundation for our youth that feeds into their future experience in the world of work. We cannot do anything about the role we have played in the academic welfare of previous students. We learn as we grow. None of us are perfect humans. We did not come into this line of work performing as perfect educators. None of us knows everything. Together, though, we know a lot. It is a 21st-century education characteristic for educators to collaborate for this very reason. Imagine the heights we can grow because we have a mindset to make the time and effort to collaborate with other experts in our field.

I suggest joining or starting professional learning communities (PLC) in elementary and high schools and faculty learning communities (FLC) at the college levels. Participation in an FLC and PLC caused me to grow immensely, making me a great benefit to my students. The years I directed my own school, the professional learning community concept was a natural process. Staff and parents met together with coffee, tea, and snacks to discuss our babies regularly. Teachers collaborated with studied and applied educational principals and instructional strategies when our babies struggled. Parents were paying tuition and expected results so they wanted to be involved in the process and we encouraged it. Discussion was open and transparent. Parents held us accountable for the academic success of their children, and we enjoyed their participation in the process. It made us feel as if we were not alone or solely responsible. As the director of the school, I was all in and fully engaged in the process. If parents did not want to be involved, the staff wanted to know why. If teachers did not participate fully, parents wanted to know why. If special resources were needed to reach a specific student we decided what we needed and figured out how to get it.

PLC practice we created was the backbone of our school. It is a practice I take with me where I teach, no matter the level. I find other faculties with whom I can discuss teaching and learning for the benefit of our students. When I was the principal of an alternative high school in the area, I embedded professional learning community time in each teacher's schedule. When I was a district leader of eight alternative high schools, I required all principals to embed time for inter-disciplinary PLC's. They were encouraged to fully understand and support the work of their PLC groups. All teachers and support staff who touched our students at the campus level participated. There was also cross-campus PLC time on in-service days. English teachers from each campus talked shop, math teachers discussed best practices, Science teachers shared lab activities, and principals shared tips for the full functioning of their individual campuses.

I sought out professors at the campus where I teach who could buy into the idea of a faculty learning community. We meet monthly to share, support, and assist one another in our reflective processes to become better at what we do. There is no ceiling for teachers, we are all lifelong learners and engaging oneself in an FLC or PLC, whatever your district calls it is transformational for teachers as well as students. The principal purpose of a PLC is highly influential for sustainability for quality teaching and learning. Every school should require teachers to participate in them and every teacher should be a part of one. Similarly, every department in a college or university should require faculty to participate in a discipline centered faculty learning community. Many colleges simulate this process with discipline-specific meetings where faculty develop strategic plans for best practices for teaching the discipline. They establish processes and protocol as well. Note, a PLC is not the place for venting and complaining about all that's wrong in education, that's a staff meeting. The focus of a PLC is solely student achievement. Participation in a PLC makes me more reflective because I have to think through why I do what I do and support my practices with research-based strategies and what I do has to make sense to my colleagues. Having to support what I do with evidence is a good reflective practice. I must be reflective as I approach my students. I must ask myself key reflective questions. The most important questions are:

- What are my strengths as an educator? Why are these your strengths?
- What are my weaknesses? How can I build upon my weaknesses?
- What are the negative experiences I provide my students and how can I avoid these pitfalls?
- What can I do to ensure I am teaching appropriately for all my students to learn?
- What must my students know in order to function well at the next level?

I believe I am a successful teacher because each time I teach a group of students, I grow my students, stretch my abilities, and I grow. They leave me better than they were when the course first started. Students often thank me for my service to their development. They thank me for my kindness, support, patience, commitment, and help. I serve urban teens and adults who are stressed by urban life. Many have been academically abused, so it is a challenge to get in their heads. In order to get the results, I seek, I strive to do these things from the first day to the last day of the course.

- Establish expectations, rather than rules
- Gain cooperation
- Build Trust
- Gently establish my Authority
- Teach Lessons from Geese to establish expectations for Scholars Circle Groups
- Provide students with an opportunity to get to know each other by engaging groups in course-related activities
- Establish authority to gain trust
- Over prepare and come to class very organized, making every minute count
- Be up. Peppy, and energetic.
- Look sharp, sound strong, firm, pleasant, reassuring, approachable and yet professional
- Share personal problems to let them know that I am not perfect.
- Allow them to empathize with me and my challenges.

My goal is to move beyond those ills that could affect my teaching and definitely does affect student learning. I put my focus on what needs to change to influence the brain of my students. Because I am an advocate for the affective domain tenets of Bloom's Taxonomy, brain-based learning come into my planning and these questions arise:

- Upon reflecting on the last class, what were its strengths and weaknesses? What needs to change?

- What instructional methods apply?
- What time should I allocate for independent reading?
- What can I do to help students comprehend and contextualize the reading?
- What is next?

Diving into the Work

    I design my Composition and Literature courses where I teach utilizing an Understanding by Design (UbD) approach. The UbD approach consists of five modules where the desired outcome is to use a multi-step process to write a five-paragraph essay which includes 3-5 citations. UbD was developed by Grant Wiggins and Jay McTighe in 1998 when the Association for Supervision and Curriculum Development published it. UbD is an approach to teaching which focuses on student achievement. My role as a facilitator in the UbD process requires that I establish clear student learning outcomes, develop constant formative assessments, and design engaging learning activities for students, keeping the "end in mind".

    In the final research project, students learn to incorporate research into their essays. They explore a community problem that affects them, write a paper outlining the problem, and explain why the problem exists in the introduction. In the body of the paper, students explore possible solutions to the problem. They incorporate researched solutions, create a survey of at least ten community stakeholders, and have an option to include the results of an interview with a community member who is an expert in providing solutions to the problem. The paper must have two to three entries on a Works Cited page and include parenthetical citations. Portions of the final module five paper are consistently and individually assessed using the online assessment journal.

    By week three or four of the semester the students work in scholars circle groups to begin the project by reading a novel. As groups read the novel they discuss the author's background, setting, theme, tone, characterization, and plot. The change I made to this module was to allow students to write this paper for the group as opposed to individual papers. This helped to lessen the course load as well as building community. Also, in module four students craft two essays about the novel. These essays are written in class so they can ask questions to ensure no ambiguity with the writing process. They can also talk to their scholars' circle group members as they write, which builds the capacity of the community. In the first essay, from module four, students include major and minor details that support the theme of the novel. The second essay in module four is a critical review where they incorporate at least one critical review from a scholarly journal, newspaper, or magazine.

    During week four consists of writing from reading selections in the textbook. Students are assigned a descriptive essay, a narrative essay, and an argumentative essay from the text. I select readings to which learners can relate. When the reading is relevant to them, they are least likely to have difficulty providing specific details and examples for their paper. They generate a three-part parallel thesis statement in the online assessment journal. Next, for each reading, learners write an essay to support the thesis. Students reported that the coursework was too heavy. So, I require students to write two of the three essays we study. They must write an argumentative essay but can choose to write either a descriptive essay or a narrative essay. Writing from these inquiries consists of writing two essays. We write a pre-essay together as a group using the projector and whiteboard in class. Each time I model the writing process I immediately see light bulbs as I observe students' body language. Afterward, students complete the muddiest point classroom assessment in the online assessment journal. Essay one is a summary response written from the topics explored early in the course, before week 5. Additionally, learners are more engaged in learning when they are the focus. Essay two is an essay outlining and describing in detail S.M.A.R.T. (smart, attainable, measurable, relevant, and time-bound) career goals and how his or her educational path relates to their goals.

Thus, the first four weeks of the semester are developed with the affective domain in mind. During these initial weeks, I attempt to get to know students and how to best serve them. The goal of this time is to motivate students in order to engage them in the learning process. Learners participate in activities and discussions which will help them explore their learning style, their own strengths, and their weaknesses as students. I understand that adults come to my course with experiential knowledge, module one is my opportunity to tap into that knowledge while providing students with opportunities to earn points towards their midterm grade at the same time. The first two weeks are focused on relationship building. The writing that occurs in week three and four occur in the online assessment journal and is about motivating topics relating to self, personal experiences, as well as personal and career goals. Motivation is a critical factor in student engagement. It is important that learners are engaged early in the course in order to reach the end successfully.

I use formative assessments to monitor my teaching and try to clearly state expectations and model them. I am open to re-teaching concepts based on the results of formative assessments either to individual students or the entire class as a whole. I study the characteristics of an adult learner and try to utilize these characteristics to set students up for success, not failure. I respect the learners who sit in front of me as the adults they are and I am prepared to learn from them as well.

Providing timely and consistent feedback to student writing is imperative to both classroom management and student's writing progress. It is critical to improving student writing. Feedback should be specific to student learning outcomes. The sooner students receive feedback that is specific the feedback (particular); the sooner they make corrections, the more powerful the learning potential. This is probably the stage of writing where my students learn the most. I follow the same three-part formula for giving feedback that I follow for correcting inappropriate behavior. I lead with something positive and complementary (authentic). Then I state those things that need to be corrected. I tell them what they did right. All my writers do something right, even in the beginning (regenerate). Too much criticism falls on deaf ears and they will not accept it as constructive criticism and shut down. It is important that the comments are authentic.

Next, if there are too many corrections I do not want to overwhelm the student, so I focus on the top three to five, depending on the student's degree of confidence (refine). If there are many corrections to be made, I make sure I tell the student ahead of time that I want them to focus on a few baby steps so they know what to expect. Much of the refining portion containing necessary corrections are written in questions. I think questions are often underestimated. Teachers tend to give answers rather than ask questions. Questioning helps to keep students engaged in the revision process. It is a proven way to stimulate the way students think about their writing. I ask for feedback regarding the contents of the syllabus at the beginning of the course and feed forward at the end of the course. This way I can make necessary and appropriate changes to the syllabus and my processes so future students are able to have a better experience. My students usually appreciate my asking for feedback and feel honored I asked for feed-forward. My feedback must be conscious, carefully planned, and well-managed.

Finally, I remind the student that I believe in their abilities and I believe they can be successful. This alone makes an impact. It is also imperative that I give feedback with an encouraging tone and body language. I smile a lot when giving feedback. My students feel welcome and open to accepting what I need to say about their writing. The one thing a teacher should never do when giving feedback is to shame a student, either verbally or in writing. The common practice of teachers shaming students is insidious. When a student is shamed he or she shuts down and mistrusts. They also learn to shame others as a result.

When we neglect to provide students with effective feedback, students work blindly and it will take longer to reach the student learning objectives successfully. As you can see, I use a partner of feedback, called feed-forward, introduced to education by Joe Hirsch leadership coach (Edutopia, 2015), to have students look ahead and aim high in their writing, keeping their eye on the course objectives and student learning outcomes as they construct their work. There six characteristics of feed-forward are illustrated by the acronym REPAIR (regenerate, expand, particular, authentic, impact, and refine), are described above, but not necessarily in that order. We know that our students need to work toward solutions and goals. Feedback should be given on an individual basis. When using a well-developed rubric, that is corrective in nature, students are able to do a self-evaluation giving themselves feedback. A clear rubric is a perfect tool that allows students to participate in the feedback process. It makes it a simple process for peer to peer feedback to happen as well. A rubric affords students the opportunity to monitor their own progress and makes feedback from other students more valuable.

Technology in the Classroom

The use of technology in the classroom is another way of preventing misbehavior in the classroom. My courses are Technology-Enhanced Courses. Students experience a combination of face to face instruction and online tools which provide reinforcement. My courses are not "flipped" in a typical manner. The "flipped" instructional strategy is a 21st-century teaching and learning strategy where instructors post video and other learning material before the lecture. I utilize the exact opposite approach. After a lecture when students learn a new skill, I post videos and other learning material to reinforce learning instead of introducing new learning. Students can use videos, PowerPoint and other interactive web tools for the classroom, sample essays and compare them to the notes they took in class. Take time to research and study Bloom's Taxonomy cognitive domain for online tools for the classroom.

Bloom's Techonomy	Look for technology so students will….
Remembering	Copy, define, locate, outline, retrieve, memorize, tabulate, bookmark, etc.
Understanding	Gather, annotate, paraphrase, predict, tag, journal, infer, interpret, etc.
Applying	Articulate, enact, display, judge, integrate, chart, examine, select, etc.
Analyzing	Organize, question, deduce, explain, mindmap, calculate, categorize, etc.
Evaluating	Editorialize, debate, predict, moderate, measure, compare, contrast, etc.
Creating	Blog, animate, solve, facilitate, build, adapt, compose, collaborate, etc.

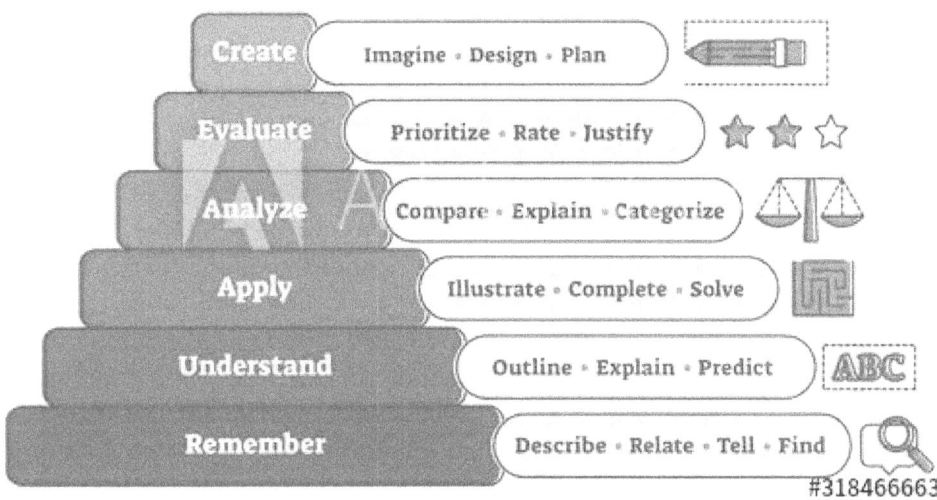
stock.adobe.com

Classroom time is spent learning, problem-solving, analyzing, asking questions, discussing, practicing, and engaging in the writing process. Therefore, students learn and relearn both inside the class and outside of class. They use videos and other course resources to reinforce learning outside of class. They learn to be independent and self-directed. Using tools available in course resources on the school's course management system, students learn to acquire study skills while they learn to master writing. Also, I encourage the use of technology in the classroom. Students can use IPads, laptops, and even cell phones with online capabilities in the classroom. I include a Technology in the Classroom policy in my course syllabus. The purpose is so students are aware that other technology, including a cell phone, is allowed in the classroom, however, solely for academic purposes only. Of course, I am forced to remind students of the technology policy, especially for cell phones, regularly. I prefer to give some students a constant reminder cell phones in the classroom are for academic purposes only, rather than not have access to technology in the classroom. There is so much to do on a cell phone in the classroom. Students can look up definitions, find synonyms, research ideas and concepts as well as learn basic grammar, punctuation, and spelling skills they may not have learned in elementary or other high school classes.

I do not understand why schools still use well thought out systems for collecting and redistributing student's phones. Yet we complain there are not enough computer labs or the computers we do have are always broken and IT still has not come to fix them yet. We complain the school does not have enough computers to go around when most students, even those in elementary school, have mini-computers in their pockets. My students write essays in Google Docs and Microsoft Word on their phones. They create slideshows, record and edit videos for projects, and conduct really good research. Although there are drawbacks to allowing them to use their cell phones, I believe the rewards are greater than the inconvenience.

Technology in the classroom allows students greater control over their learning process. I am able to employ this technology in the classroom motivation approach, which changes attitudes about learning, establishes clear perceptions about learning, and alter values, using a technology-enhanced approach. The trajectory is implementing teaching and learning in a way that conveys each student's confidence in his or her ability to learn. This way my respect for students becomes more apparent to each. Allowing students to use cell phones, Ipads, and laptops in the classroom removes the power struggle I use to face in trying to get students to turn cell phones off and tuck them away with their personal belongings. I do not have to engage in this power struggle any longer and students feel I am approachable and respectful to them as learners. Building relationships are necessary for both classroom management and student success. Allowing technology in the classroom helps in building relationships.

To help eliminate the digital divide, I model and demonstrate computer applications for them regularly. I have students who have apps on their phones that allow them to write an essay in class, upload it to the course management system, and view the feedback generated by the course management app immediately. If your school district does not utilize a course management system or you need to supplement the features of the one you use simply do a Google search for 101 free Web 2.0 and Web 3.0 online Teaching Tools or free course management resources. If your school does not have enough technology to go around, take the lead and seek out funding for technology specifically for your classroom. Collaborate with your professional learning community and write a proposal for a few laptop carts that can be your PLC or FLC and share. Your learning community can also organize a fundraiser for the same purpose. "Where there is a will, there's a way." I know it is not your job to provide resources for your students, but it is your job to reach them. The young people we teach are digital natives. Incorporating technology is one way we can reach them and engage them in the learning process. You do not have to do it alone. Organizing other teachers around you and sharing the responsibility for the incorporation of responsible use of technology is an extremely important skill the students need in the 21st century.

21st Century Learning Skills

Inquiry-based Instruction is a holistic approach that involves technology, collaboration, and reflection to develop ownership by the student in their educational process. It empowers the student with skills to aid in their real-life journey. These are important skills needed in the 21st century:
- Communications
- Preparation
- Understand Protocol
- Organization
- Team-building
- Self-correction and self-management
- Self-Reflection
- Respect and trust while learning.

6
Critical Relationships

Preparing Students for a Scholar's Circle

Teacher-student relationships and student-student relationships are both critical. I make it clear to learners that they are expected to participate in all class activities, submit all assignments and be an active member of a Scholars Circle. I also explain that each Scholars Circle member is expected to be a part of all group discussions and projects. Scholars Circle group study offers several advantages, including a student's ability to gain a deeper understanding of class material. Most students are cooperative after the first two days of orientation activities. I have discovered that many students learn best when engaged with peers and when the environment is collaborative, engaging, positive and encouraging. Research shows that students who make friends with other students and study with other students are more likely to be successful in school. Therefore, I require all students to participate in a Scholar's Circle.

Getting to know each other is the first step in establishing functional Scholar's Circle groups. This part of the day one and two orientation process. You can buy a book on team building activities and do a search for a list online. Team building activities are powerful tools I use to develop Scholar's Circle groups with few dysfunctions; so, I take my time and select appropriate activities for the results I want. These activities bring students together and encourage them to collaborate. The fun and laughter that is created in team-building games helps lighten the classroom environment, builds a team spirit and encourages camaraderie. Team building exercises are motivational and make students feel comfortable so when the hard discussions happen, they happen. Students begin to work with peers in communication, solving problems, giving feedback, and resolving project conflict. It takes time in the beginning of the semester to build groups into working teams. Usually after the bonding from completing the campus scavenger hunt ant the syllabus scavenger hunt groups are ready to begin building Scholars Circle teams by creating a mission, logo, as well as group values, roles, and group protocol. These front load activities, about two sessions, bond the Scholar's Circle groups fostering the team connection necessary for class activities for the remainder of the semester or year. The time spent front loading is well worth the time and effort. When we do not take this time, I am always very sorry we didn't.

Students learn rules and best practices for working together with our study of "Lessons from Geese" was transcribed from a speech given by Angeles Arrien at the 1991 Organizational Development Network and is based on the work of Milton Olson. Initial activities to build group camaraderie include Lessons from Geese, creating a vision and developing a mission statement for the group. Scholar's Circle groups also spend quality time creating a trademark. These activities help to "brand" the group and build them into functional teams. When I do not take time to build Scholar's Circle groups into working teams, I spend the semester resolving the conflict for dysfunctional teams who do not work well together. I also teach students how to engage in small discussions and set ground rules. In setting grounds rules students are grouped into groups of 3-5 to share notes, individually and silently write down recollections of their best and worst discussion experiences, record specific things which made discussions either satisfying and frustrating, brainstorm specific things students do to make discussions go well, brainstorm specific things teachers do to make discussions go well, and share ways that cause a discussion to be frustrating.

As ground rules are set, I organize the initial small group discussion activity to create an environment where students feel respected before groups begin to discuss course material and readings. I ask groups to convert the most frequently mentioned features to specific behaviors that should be encouraged or discouraged on newsprint or post it. Then I provide newsprint or poster size post-it papers and markers. Finally, I allow students to share with the large group for discussion.

Many instructors are hesitant to conduct class discussions because they can be unpredictable hard to manage, and pose a potential challenge. Students often get overly excited and loud, unruly arguments could occur quite easily. On the other hand, there are usually some students that are withdrawn and never say anything at all; while there are students who dominate the discussion. Small group discussion has amazing benefits though. They enforce active learning, promote deep thinking and a sense of community, and build accountability for students. During robust and engaging small group discussions students expand their opinions, defend their positions, and sometimes even change their beliefs. The six discussions I use most often are Conver-Stations (also called Rotation Stations), Circle of Voices, Socratic Circle, One the Spot Thought, Jigsaw, and Think-Pair-Share. You can easily check Stanford University's Teaching Commons, The Teaching Center at Washington University or Yale Center for Teaching and Learning to get instructions for these strategies. I created videos of these strategies and use them in workshops.

At times, I see myself as an actress on stage during the first two days of class. I try to hook them, grab their attention, and begin to develop a working relationship with them. I tell my students a difficult story about myself, this seems to break the ice very quickly, it makes me a bit vulnerable, but it draws my students into my space and creates respect and trust. My goal is to sell students on my syllabus, my expectations for their success, my belief that they can be successful, and the work we have ahead. I am responsible for making my audience feel comfortable with my syllabus. I help them feel as if they are able to reach the high expectations set within the syllabus while promoting self-responsibility. I am connecting those difficult components: student, teacher, and subject. I put time into cultivating a professional appearance, conduct, communication techniques, attitude, voice, and smile as I teach the syllabus. This prevents students from being fearful and uncertain.

By the end of the second day of class, students know that I am approachable and that I want to help them be successful. They understand that I have high expectations but I am also more than willing to help them fulfill those expectations. At this point, students are ready to read and sign the Learner Contract because they have gained a willingness to listen and comprehend what I am teaching. The syllabus symbolizes an obligatory contract. I seal the agreement of classroom participation by having students sign and date the Learner Contract located at the end of the syllabus. My intent is for the contract to confirm students read the syllabus, understand its contents, ask questions when they do not understand, and agree to do their best to abide by the contract. Of course, there are instances where students are not able to abide by the contract. In this case, students are able to discuss the hardship with me privately. I am approachable and flexible when students have extreme challenges and I will negotiate terms on an individual basis.

Establishing Authority and Rapport

In building healthy professional relationships with learners, I have to establish that I am the authority in the classroom. I do this by setting high expectations, goals, and objectives for the course, and also establishing assignment deadlines. This step helps to establish class comportment throughout the course. Good classroom comportment is also established when I teach procedures, standards, and norms. This includes letting students know how to ask for my help while in class as well as outside of class. Establishing norms also includes my expectations for homework and how to submit it and how students should function when working in Scholars Circle Groups. You will see more of this in the section on planning using the E.N.G.AG.E. Action Plan worksheet. Scholars Circle is a group of student scholars who make a commitment to study and work together and help one another pass a course.

I strongly believe at-risk students learn more from an instructor who has a passion for his or her subject. I utilize the first class to introduce myself and clearly express my passion for teaching and being a writer. In my approach and delivery, I strive to reach my students and excite them about the upcoming classes. In order to establish authority and build rapport, I maintain a professional appearance, practice good conduct, and utilize clear and firm communication techniques. I also maintain a positive and pleasant attitude. To build rapport, I share my truths, values, the barriers that I have overcome and how I have overcome them. I also share a few current struggles and barriers. When students leave class on days one and two, they know that I am approachable and that I want to help them be successful. They understand that I have high expectations but also know that I am more than willing to help them fulfill those expectations.

In the week one orientation process, I observe students carefully with the intent to be alert to early signs of students who may have difficulty. I also aid and referrals to help students address their issues and challenges. Students are required to create a profile within our course management system as orientation homework. This profile includes a picture of themselves, a completed learning style assessment, and their career goals. I carefully review the student profiles and match the profile with the students I observe in class on day one and two. I continuously scan the classroom observing students in order to recognize and identify students who may have limitations in the areas of writing, reading, following instructions, and behavior. I demonstrate my authority by referring to all students, who exhibit behavior or academic challenges, to their advisors for appropriate help before it affects their class standing.

When I take attendance, I work to put a name to the faces of learners whom I observe may have academic difficulty or any student who could possibly be challenged behaviorally. I make notations on the attendance sheet to keep track of my observations. The students who I identify as most likely to have a behavior problem are the ones I target to build and encourage first. I am aware that students may be under significant stress, so I avoid confrontations and I am patient and considerate of such students. Within the orientation process, I make sure students know the location of the Wellness Center and its purposes. I spend time explaining the purposes of the Disabilities Office and its location. I also make students aware of the Writing Center and other academic support services available to them by engaging them in a campus-specific scavenger hunt where students locate offices and collect information for all offices that offer student support and resources. I am responsible for making my audience feel comfortable and help them gain confidence that they are able to reach the high expectations I sets while promoting self-responsibility. My approach is also geared to prevent students from being fearful, timid and uncertain. Managing students is more effective when it is preventative and begins on the first day and the classroom management plan is simple. I strive to accomplish this simplicity with the teaching of my syllabus. I develop my syllabus with the intent to ensure a professional yet engaging teacher-student relationship.

My method for presenting my syllabus is an important part of this process. Day one and two are set aside for an intense, loud, fun, collaborative orientation. The syllabus design and the orientation activities provide that link. They are my first attempt to build a good rapport with my students. I tell a difficult personal story to help build trust. I intermingle personal stories into my presentation of the syllabus, as well as through the semester so that many students get to know me and can see me as a person. I also create easy and quick assignments pertaining to syllabus comprehension. These assignments allow my students to get an early understanding of classroom achievement.

My process for teaching the syllabus during orientation is imperative. My syllabus is my way of beginning the facilitation of teaching and learning. As I get to know my students I also build my skills in developing instructional strategies that will assist the students in developing metacognitive skills. I strive to set the class up for success from the very beginning and to discover their individual learning styles so I have a general idea about how to reach them. I teach the syllabus using a lively and active slide presentation. Included in the slide is a short video clip explaining the importance of a syllabus and table talk opportunities, a video clip about working in scholars' groups, and good study habits. Embedded in the presentation are fun activities allowing students to get to know me and I get to know them. I spend the first day teaching the syllabus using a pleasant smile, and approachable attitude, and bare facts from the syllabus in an engaging slide presentation using a projector and screen creating a multi-media environment. The presentation helps to ensure I reach the various learning needs of the students before me. I allow students to ask questions gaining clarity on any issue raised or component of the syllabus. The first group task, part of the orientation activities, is to review the syllabus in order to complete the Campus Scavenger Hunt, in which students review the contents of the syllabus to answer questions. By the beginning of week three, after the focus was on students getting to know one another, gaining information about peers so they can make informed decisions, and beginning to get connected to the work ahead.

Inquiry-based instruction is the first step to connecting students to real work situations. Every time students are pushing through obstacles they are verbally encouraged to push through even more. Grit in action happens when students are given time to reflect upon their work either verbally or in writing. This helps them connect their values to the task to infuse new energy and Reflection time helps them to think about their own values and how they apply to their work causing them to do better work. Students experience deep learning when connected to projects and assignments, developing grit. It builds grit when they work through challenges, never give up, and use feedback to improve. It is effective training that teaches them how to constructively work with their peers. Inquiry-based learning is a true form of engaging learning activities that move the learning from "guided inquiry" to "open inquiry." All my projects are designed to include reading and research. Students are encouraged to engage themselves in the reading, annotate it, and look up words they do not know or are unsure about.

They are encouraged to ask and answer questions about the reading as they read that push them to think about what they know and need to know. These methods of active reading help them to connect to the reading recognize patterns and new possibilities. As I design each question, I pose several open-ended questions to help them draw out their thinking, rethink ideas, draw new conclusions, or support old ideas. I encourage students to take risks and not be afraid to be wrong. There is a lot to be learned while correcting errors and poor thinking. I encourage students to be active participants in their learning, rather than mere participants.

Reflection is also encouraged in students as reflecting is good for both teachings as well as learning. Reflecting and questioning help to deepen independent thinking and increase learning. Questions may include: What are your thoughts? What do you think about that? What information did you read to base your conclusion? What did you already know about the subject that could help you? Can you tell us more about that? What do you think you can add to this information? Can you explain further? What's next? How are you going to handle this? Let's explore it further? What else do you think we need to know? How do you think you are growing in this subject? What have you learned so far? How are you managing what you have learned? Open-ended questions help to scaffold information and help propel students forward to deeper learning and gaining expertise. This helps students to think. To think is the process of asking and answering questions then connecting them to the content and context. Content is expressed in writing, speech or any other form of art or media. Context refers to a specific section of a written text or an oral speech that immediately precedes or follows a word or passage that clarifies its meaning.

Technology allows students to access their work from anywhere and anytime with the internet connection. Connectivism permits students to interact with peers within and outside of the school setting. It connected both the school as a whole and my students to other schools within the city and out of the city. In many cases, connectivism connected my students with experts in the field within the scope of the project. It connected us to others internationally, using technology to open our methods of research and presentation.

7
Managing Counterproductive Behavior

I bring student development strategies with me to both the secondary and higher education classroom from my experience as a district leader of an alternative secondary school network. Closely observing body language helps me to identify possible disruptive students whom I target for building using the 10:2 approach. I target disruptive and at-risk students and keep track of my interactions with them. My goal is to spend 10 minutes with a disruptive student at least twice or 2 minutes ten times. During the ten- or two-minute intervals, I smile at the student and tell him or her things that will build his or her esteem. I build the student by complementing their efforts and progressive actions that align with course expectations. I find something to compliment them on, even if it is only congratulating them for attending the class that day. I may compliment them on minor things like spelling a word correctly, by using an appropriate MLA or APA heading or skipping lines in their work. Most of the time I can find something the student has done to earn a compliment. Over a few class sessions, I observe their classroom comportment transforming and, in most cases, clearly see them following protocol more effectively.

I utilize a restorative approach to classroom discipline, which is based on the 4 R's: respect, responsibility, relationship building, and relationship-repairing. A restorative approach does not focus on punitive practices; rather, it is based on mediation. It is an approach to classroom discipline that employs the creation of a physical, and especially an emotionally safe environment for students to grow, blossom and thrive. This restorative approach begins with me as an instructor and facilitator. I must be a model for restorative behavior at the very beginning of the course. Otherwise, the semester will be rocky and very stressful. In this case, students may or may not meet student learning outcomes.

I monitor my interactions with disruptive students, especially those who are troubled, at-risk, or disruptive. During the first few weeks of class, these students are my target and I keep an index card in my pocket with a number representing that student in case my card falls and is seen by students. I do not want to embarrass a student by having his or her name on a card for all to see. I put a tear on the top of the card for every positive interaction and a tear on the bottom of the card for every negative interaction. When I get back to my office I can see the ratio of interactions I had with the student. This is the same method I use when I target students using the 10:2 approach. According to research by Sprick, Garrison, and Howard my ratio of interaction should be 3:1. For every one negative interaction I have with one of the students targeted, I need to intentionally have three positive interactions. Dealing with the affective domain, students remember how I make them feel. I keep this in mind as I interact with students.

My strategy is based on the work of psychologist Alfred Adler's approach. He says when we feel encouraged, we feel capable and appreciated and generally act in a cooperative way. The opposite occurs when we feel inept and unappreciated. This is why during the first few days, I strategically and purposefully monitor my interactions with potentially disruptive or possible at-risk or learners. I do this without their knowledge. I attempt to correct disruptive behavior fluently using a calm and respectful tone. I pre-discuss the behavior with the student before correcting it in private. I try to be brief and consistent, using short one-liners followed by an encouraging statement and "I am sure you will be successful in this course." Prevention is key. I try to be observant, circulating the classroom. I find it impossible to teach this demographic while sitting down. When a student seems to be getting reading to get on his or her disruptive path, I try to recognize it then I try to appeal to the relationship we have built and used humor if possible.

10 Day Classroom Management Study

I managed two different alternative high school networks in Chicago at different times in my career. At the beginning of a school year and semester, when new students enrolled, student behavior could be very overwhelming and extremely stressful. We could not teach without first targeting inappropriate behaviors and then taking the time to transform those behaviors. Students were typically at risk of failure, which was why they were enrolling in our networks in the first place. They were students who did not function well in public or charter high schools because of attendance, low test scores, too many holes in their academic knowledge, poor grade point averages, failing grades, or at-risk behavior. The student body was students who had failed, often miserably, academically. Many had already been in and out of our city's juvenile detention center. Albeit some students had good literacy skills, high absenteeism from school, poor home conditions, and homelessness became insurmountable barriers they were unable to overcome.

Our alternative school networks were their last chance to acquire academic success. The responsibility of administration and faculty was to afford these students the opportunity to change their life's circumstances without judgment, but with as much care and love as possible. Believe me, in many cases, this was very difficult. It was often a painful challenge. Despite the looming challenges, my goal was to offer my students an alternative to what they were accustomed to for a more hopeful future.

I began my journey with these challenging students by building their self-esteem and belief in what was possible. As a change agent, I began encouraging them on the first day I met them, usually at registration. As the administrator, I only hired faculty and staff who could also help provide the help and encouragement our students needed with no judgment regarding their past. Hiring the appropriate faculty and staff were key elements for making a positive impact on our student body. Using the professional learning community model, we established protocols for all school wide and classroom activities. With procedural safeguards in place, we were able to enforce our expectations from the first day of school. We 'targeted' students with at-risk behavior immediately and began to treat them warmly; identify their strengths; compliment them on these strengths; identify their academic, independent, and frustration levels; engrain our high expectations, and build their self-esteem.

Many of our students left home without eating a balanced breakfast; which prompted us to begin their day with breakfast. Another effective paradigm shift to change mindsets and behaviors was to replace the traditional bell to alert student movement between classes with positive music. We believed music to be an effective tool for changing the culture and climate of our school. The 10:2 behavior management strategy I employed in these alternative high school networks worked so well, I decided to employ them in the community college classrooms. In addition, this reveals an 'at ease' yet, effective approach that allows the teacher-student relationship to bond with appropriate diplomacy.

I identified ten disruptive students from one of my English courses, where thirty-four students were enrolled, during a 16 or 12-week long course. The objective was to alter adverse behavior early in the semester; therefore, *verbal praise* was used as the variable. On Day one of the study, the variable was used for the controlled group (e.g., ten off-task students). I spoke the *verbal praise* softly to avoid other students hearing me, so as not to embarrass the targeted students. On Day two of the study, the controlled group was not given the variable, instead, I simply circulated the room. As I circulated the room the controlled group continued to talk while I lectured, while the non-controlled group was on task. I noticed my targeted students were not as responsive as they were Day one having been given the variable, verbal praise.

The variable was applied using a formula with three parts.

- Part 1 - "I really like the way you..." (to build self-confidence)
- Part 2 - "I am certain you can pass the posttest when you focus on..." (to identify the progress made thus far)
- Part 3 - I think you can do really well in this class. (to keep focused on successful completion)

Behavior Management Analysis: Controlled Group

The purpose of this behavior management study is to use '*verbal praise*' to redirect students who are sometimes resistant to the learning process. I observe student behavior and body language on day one to identify students who may have the potential to cause a classroom management challenge. I use '*verbal praise*' within the first two weeks of the course, in order to redirect inappropriate behavior.

Student A

Summary: Student A was one of the ten students in the controlled group, a 21-year-old female, Hispanic, single mother who earned her GED two years prior to current enrollment in the course. This was her 2nd attempt at the developmental course prior to entering college-level courses.

Rationale: The major problems with Student A was disruptive talking during classroom instruction, not following instructions, exhibiting disruptive behavior that disturbs cooperative classroom conduct. This behavior was mainly attributed to insecurity or a feeling of inept knowledge of acquired skills. Student A's adverse behavior interrupted the instructional flow of the class. She talked during lecture and class instruction which left her less informed as to what and how to accomplish class objectives and complete assignments.

Findings: On Day one the student responded to '*verbal praise*' intermittently. By Day five of the study, student A stopped talking during class altogether and no longer disrupted her group with unrelated comments, nor did she disrupt the class during the rest of the course. I continued to apply the variable ('*verbal praise*', using an encouraging statement) intermittently during the entire 10 days. The student began communicating valuable input to group work on day five as well. She was no longer a behavior challenge by the end of the study. I noticed the female student's intent was intimidation. My purpose was to avoid getting in a power struggle with the student. I had to approach Student A slowly, calmly, and immediately while the behavior was in progress.

Student B

Summary: A 19-year-old African American male, who graduated from an alternative high school. He was a first-time college student. Student B was in the controlled group.

Rationale: Student B's behavior was best met with a formula of patience, firm intent, coupled with the variable of immediate '*verbal praise*'. My response had to remain completely firm without aggression, forcefulness, or disrespect. It was imperative that my expression of nonverbal body language was not antagonistic. This allowed Student B to quiet himself immediately and remain focused on the learning objectives and goals of the day.

Findings: On Day one and Day two, the variables had no apparent impact. The conclusive findings in this study point to Male Student B exhibiting disrespect and defiance to authority figures. His constant talking demonstrated disregard to direct instruction as well as group dynamics. However, on Day Three, there was a sudden shift in his behavior. He stopped talking and disrupting for the duration of the course, yet he avoided eye contact with me. I continued to apply the variable, occasionally, to reinforce the desired behavior though he was quiet, he seemed passive-aggressive because he did not contribute to his group nor whole class activities. Though there was a shift in his behavior, the shift did not affect his academic efforts. I took this to mean his behavior was still non-compliant. However, on Day Six, he began to make eye contact with me and engage in his group dynamics by adding to activities and discussions.

Student C

Summary: An 18-year-old African American female, who has recently graduated from high school and is a first-time college student-athlete. Student C was also part of the controlled group.

Rationale: The major problems with Student C were tardiness and absence, disruptive talking during classroom instruction, exhibiting disruptive behavior that disturbs cooperative classroom conduct. The problem observed was that because the student was tardy, she attempted to ask students what she missed and became offended and irritated when I asked her to stop.

Findings: On day one with this student no '*verbal praise*' was applied to Student C. It was my practice to circulate the room as I lectured. When I noticed the student's behavior and her methods for finding out what was missed because of tardiness, I prepared five post-it notes before class. As I circulated, I walked to the student's table and put a sticky note on her notebook with these instructions, "I'm glad you made it. Do your best to figure out where we are and what you missed without interrupting the flow of the class. You did not miss much and you can find the place on your own by listening carefully and being observant of the reading. I am certain you will complete this class successfully." The first time I did not make eye contact or smile and noticed an attitude developing. She appeared surprised and grimaced a bit. She asked the two people on either side her as soon as I walked away. I continued to circulate. When I made my way back to her, I gave her a second note, but I made eye contact and smiled.

On day three, when I noticed Student C coming in the door, I made my way to her desk, handed her a fourth note as she sat down, still tardy. I asked her to see me after class. My purpose was to talk to her about being tardy. I discovered during the individual conference, Student C was tardy because she was a caretaker for an ill grandmother. I simply paraphrased the instructions in the note showing understanding and compassion. I never approached her about her tardiness since it was the talking which caused the disturbance. A '*verbal praise*' was applied each time she made it to class, whether tardy or not for the duration of the study. After the first two weeks of sticky notes, she even whispered, "phew, it was tough" or "I am glad I made it too" and eventually, "thank you, professor". Ultimately, the student simply smiled or shook her head yes. Student C's attendance grew more consistent. After week four she was only tardy occasionally.

Interpretation of the behavior management study

'*Verbal praise*' has a positive impact on successful teaching and learning. The simple behavior modification tactic is a non-aggressive approach applied with patience, intent, and firmness. The lack of reciprocated aggression allowed the '*verbal praise*' formula to be a success. Perhaps, calm and patience from the teacher may be the most difficult task. However, the results out weight any difficulty the teacher may have. It is calm which causes the student to respond, and students respond immediately to encouragement. Encouragement redirects most students almost immediately. It appeared to me, over the course of the study, that males are a bit easier to redirect than females.

Setting Limits and Establishing Consequences

It is not all learners who are confrontational or who need intervention. However, even in adult education, there are students who need intervention and who can be confrontational. Setting limits may be one of the most effective tools I use to promote positive behavior changes for my students. Setting reasonable limits for students who could pose a classroom management challenge is one way of preventing conflict and avoiding confrontation. When students understand that there are limits to their behavior helps the entire class feel safe. Setting limits helps learners, especially at-risk learners, to make appropriate choices. It is the unprepared student who is unfocused and at-risk of being a behavior challenge. In this case, it is important that I not lose control by entering into a power struggle with the student. I also need to be careful of both my nonverbals and verbal interaction with this student because the student will easily shift from the real issue to a power struggle. I need to make sure the messages exchanged remain positive as I attempt to redirect him or her. Setting a limit is not the same as issuing an ultimatum. Setting limits is not making threats. Setting limits offer valid choices with consequences.

Limit setting example

Incorrect: "Stop talking and get busy with your assignment now. If you do not want to work then leave or I will call security and have you escorted out! "

Correct: "Please try to focus on the assignment. If you finish it in class then I will give you 5 extra credit points. It's your decision. "

Correct: "Please try to focus on the assignment. If you finish, in class then you won't have to finish it for homework. It's your choice."

Correct: "Please try to focus on the assignment. If you finish in 15 minutes then you can discuss the next task with your Scholars Circle members. You know two or three heads are better than one." You decide.

8

Reflective Teaching & Learning

Planning is making every minute count and reflecting on it as a facilitator ahead of time. Planning well is the first line of defense for effective classroom management. It is important to establish high expectations for student achievement. Strong classroom management also requires a teacher's ability to set procedures with intended outcomes in mind so that students understand how to carry out tasks independently. Effective teachers establish the protocol to head off behavior challenges while planning thoroughly to make an impact on successful teaching and learning. Good teachers reflect upon their plans often and revise them when necessary. When teachers plan well, good classroom management is the result. It keeps the class organized and keeps teaching and learning on track, thus ensuring more teaching and learning occurs and less effort is needed to "manage" students.

Being a reflective educator is imperative for successful planning and effective classroom management. Everything that occurs in a classroom is an opportunity for reflective learning. Reflective teaching means planning what you do in a classroom, revisiting your plan constantly, thinking about why you do it, thinking about whether or not it works, and changing it when necessary. Reflective teaching, serious thinking, is a necessary process for self-observation and self-evaluation, with student achievement being first in mind. Reflective teachers model the behavior for students so that reflection becomes a habit of mind and is linked to their experiences constructively. Reflection is good for teaching as well as learning because it encourages comprehension and higher-order thinking based on prior knowledge and current experiences.

Constructivism

Constructivism is most effective when reflection exists. Constructivism is an Inquiry-based instructional method that connects the student to real-life experiences and develops real-life results or solutions. Constructivism according to authors J.G.Brooks and M.G.Brooks state there are 12 descriptors which encourage and ensure the students' role in their own understanding. Utilizing these descriptors, I became a facilitator of information rather than one who presents and tells. In this way, my role as a traditional teacher was transformed. While I forged my personal interpretation in my quest to become a constructivist teacher. Constructivist teachers:

- Encourage and accept student autonomy and initiative (connections amongst ideas and concepts).
- Use raw data and primary sources, along with manipulatives, interactive and physical materials (abstractions generated through interaction with ideas).
- When framing tasks, use cognitive terminology such as "classify," "analyze", "predict", and "create" (these words affect our way of thinking then our actions).
- Allow student responses to drive lessons (projects), shift instructional strategies, and alter the content (teachable moments and student interest, experiences).
- Inquire about students' understanding of concepts before sharing their own understanding of those concepts.
- Encourages students to engage in dialogue, both with the teacher and with one another (present their ideas and listen to others and reflect).

- Encourages student inquiry by asking thoughtful, open-ended questions and encouraging students to ask questions of each other (allowing for the development of thoughtful, complex challenging questions from their own experiences and understanding of events and phenomena).
- Seek elaboration of students' initial responses.
- Engages students in experiences that might engender contradictions to their initial hypotheses and then encourages discussion.
- Allow wait time after posing questions (questions posed by the teacher may not be the questions heard by the students, use the small group setting then move into a large group setting).
- Provide time for students to construct relationships and create metaphors. (metaphors help to understand complex issues in a holistic way and time is needed to see if it works).
- Nurture students' natural curiosity through frequent use of the learning cycle. This is a science education model published by Atkin and Karplus (1962). The study was focused on self-regulation in the learning process. Curriculum development and instruction were illustrated by a three-step cycle.
    - The discovery phase is when the teacher provides an open-ended opportunity with selected purposeful materials to generate questions and hypotheses.
    - Concept introduction lessons that focus students' questions, new vocabulary, framing their lab experiences.
    - Concept application completes the cycle after one or more iterations of the discovery-concept introduction sequence which focuses on new problems with the potential of developing a new look.

The Importance of Feedback and Feed forward

As an educator of the constructivist process, I learned to understand the need for "feedback". Feedback should increase productivity and team harmony. Feedback should also be goal-referenced; tangible and transparent; actionable; user-friendly (specific and personalized); timely; on-going; and consistent. Feedback should answer three central questions for students from their point of view:
1. What knowledge or skills form my learning target for this lesson or project?
2. How close am I/we to mastering them?
3. What do we need to do next to close the gap?

Moss and Brookhart (2009) suggest that "Feedback", better coined "Feed forward" shares five characteristics:
1. Focus on success criteria from the learning target for today's lesson.
2. Describes exactly where the student is in relation to the criteria.
3. Provides a next step strategy that the student should use to improve or learn more.
4. Arrives when the student has the opportunity to use it.

5. Delivered in just the right amount, not so much that it overwhelms, but not so little that it stops short of a useful explanation or suggestion.

I learned the value of providing feedback to my students, as they developed their projects, on a regular basis. Project-based Instruction is an active tool that can utilize feed forward capabilities; that is, information and images related to what can be done more correctly in the future. According to Joe Hirsch (Edutopia, 2015), there are six characteristics of feed forward illustrated by the acronym REPAIR (regenerate, expand, particular, authentic, impact, and refine). We know that our students need to work toward solutions and goals; therefore, like formative assessment, feedback should be given on an individual basis. Feedback is for the "right now" in the project aiding the goal-direction of the project. According to (Hattie, 2009), Feedback should answer three central questions for students from their point of view.

1. What knowledge or skills form my learning target this lesson or project?
2. How close am I, or my group, to mastering them?
3. What do I, or my group need to do next to close the gap?

Moss & Brookhart (2009) states that "feedback" and "feed forward" share five major characteristics: Both "feedback" and "feed forward"

1. Focus on success criteria from the student learning outcome for today's lesson.
2. Describe exactly where the student is in relation to the outcome.
3. Provide a next step strategy that the student should use to improve or learn even more.
4. Both are fulfilled and act effectively when the student has the opportunity to use the information.
5. Both are delivered at just the right pace so as not to overwhelm students, but not so little that it stops short of a useful explanation or suggestion.

"Every truth has four corners: as a teacher, I give you one corner, and it is for you to find the other three." .... Confucius

To sum it up, becoming a constructivist teacher is embracing the way in which people learn. True constructivist studies her students, to be an effective teacher a constructivist embraces teaching and learning of students and on the flip side her own teaching and learning as well. In other words, students learn as I teach; while I learn that my students teach me. "Once teachers are exposed to these practices, they enthusiastically experiment with constructivist pedagogy until it becomes part of the very fabric of their classrooms" (Brooks. 1999, p. 101). I am not one to resist constructivist pedagogy. I am not committed to any traditional approach. I am most concerned about student learning. Whatever I can do to ensure the students in front of me learn, I do. I do not need to be overly concerned about classroom control because I front the load the semester with instructing students about my expectations, building relationships, and behavior management. I am not afraid of learning will erode my control. Rather, learning is the control and I am completely willing to give control of my classroom to learning by allowing student responses to drive my planning and my implementation learning. There are times when learning is quiet. There are times when learning is busy and loud. There are times when learning is independent or collaborative. These expectations are determined in my micro-planning.

9

E.N.G.A.G.E Action Plan

Planning to teach using E.N.G.A.G.E. is restorative and promotes active learning.

The E.N.G.A.G.E. action plan is a restorative approach that employs active learning as a process whereby students engage in activities, such as reading, writing, discussion, or problem-solving that promote analysis, synthesis, and evaluation of class content. Using the E.N.G.A.G.E. action plan when planning lessons helps to combat counterproductive behavior. Active learning means students engage with the material, participate in the class, and collaborate with each other. Engaging students in active learning deters behavior problems. Using the E.N.G.A.G.E. action plan for developing lessons helps to build healthy classroom communities and decrease antisocial behavior, as well as helps to build healthy relationships in the classroom. Don't expect your students simply to listen and memorize; instead, have them help demonstrate a process, analyze an argument, or apply a concept to a real-world situation. Using active learning as a restorative practice includes the use of both informal and formal planning processes to proactively prevent behavior problems or conflict by building relationships and ensuring student engagement.

A classroom where students are participating in active learning is vastly different from the traditional classroom where the teacher lectures and students are expected to sit still for long periods of time, take notes, and absorb the information. While being engaged in active learning, students listen for shorter periods of time and take notes. They then discuss or debate in small groups, propose opposing viewpoints, evaluate related ideas, practice individually, write or create, and complete various other activities. The students then apply what they have heard either in the lecture or based on what they read. Active learning engages students in "doing" and thinking creatively and critically about "doing." When I create, implement, monitor, and assess what students are "doing", I allow them to select a subtopic with a theme I select. This process of having them make decisions about what they learn and how they use the new knowledge causes them to see the information I teach as more valuable. I am ensuring learning, increasing student investment, increasing their motivation, and enforcing excellent performance. When I invite my students to be actively participatory in the learning environment, giving clear instructions, I simultaneously create an environment conducive to active learning. This is the lesson plan format I use to engage my students.

E.N.G.A.G.E. Students in Active learning

Exercise

- Describe the exercise.
- What is the activity?
- What is the expected product?

Writing points: various activities that occur in the course of a day.

Nurture

- How will the teacher nurture students during the exercise?
- How will the teacher ensure they receive the support and help they need to successfully complete the exercise?
- How do students get the teacher's attention to get their questions answered?
- What do students do in case they have to wait to get the teacher's response to their questions?
- How do students get the motivation to complete the exercise successfully?
- How does the teacher create opportunities to build students up?
- Writing points: expectations for student behavior while the student is circulating the room.

Grade

- How will the exercise be assessed?
- What are the expectations for grades using a grading rubric?
- How can students earn an A?
- How can students earn a B?
- Why might a student earn a C for the exercise?
- Why might a student earn a D for the exercise?
- Why might a student earn an F for the exercise?
- What formative assessments will the teacher use to improve the exercise?
- What Web 2.0 tools will be needed to monitor and assess the exercise?
- Writing points: development of rubrics.

Action
- What are acceptable actions and behaviors for the exercise?
- What actions and behaviors show students are participating responsibly and fully?
- How long will the activity last?
- How should students manage their time?
- What Web 2.0 tools will students use to complete the activity?
- How are students expected to participate in the exercise?
- What should students do when they are done?
- Writing Points: expectations.

Genuineness

- What is honest?
- What is integrity?
- What is true?
- What is forthright?
- What is plagiarizing?
- What is cheating?
- Writing points: integrity in student work.

Exchange
- Can students talk or exchange ideas with a partner?
- Or group?
- For how long?
- How often?
- For what reason?
- Writing Points: student collaboration.

Case Studies

Case Study 1

You're in the middle of a PowerPoint or slide presentation for your class. Students are following along and taking brief notes. What you haven't yet realized is that one student is setting small paper balls on the head of a student directly in front of him. Others frequently pick on the student in front of them. The students seated close by have seen what is happening and are doing their best to muffle their laughter. You notice the snickering, though you are unable to identify the participants. **How would you quell the brewing potential problem?**

    My approach to classroom management is first preventive, then restorative. On Day one, I teach expectations for all classroom activities. I teach students how to E.N.G.A.G.E. themselves in activities. Consequently, students learn what behavior is expected during individual work, group work when they first arrive in class. I arrive in the classroom before my students to prepare my mind and complete any last-minute organizing. When students arrive, I greet them with a smile and warm greeting and observe their mood. Because I have formed a relationship with them, they do not usually mind if I ask questions about how they feel or what is going on in their lives. I remind them to tell me if they need a quiet moment during the lesson or activity. I reassure them that I am there to help them get through the day.

    I know when "Charles" will possibly display inappropriate behavior and he knows I know. I can subtly raise my eyebrows at him as I ask an intriguing question or place a warm and gentle hand on the shoulder of "Tammie" as I progress around the room to prevent her from attempting to break "John's" concentration during an independent activity. In this case, I would see the first spitball on the floor. I would recognize the culprit's behavior as he tries to hide his hand. I would observe the students around him as they attempt to quell their laughter. I would not interrupt my teaching to highlight this inappropriate behavior. I would instead target these students with questions about the lesson or repeat the instructions for the independent activity in the form of questions. Knowing that the student who is being bullied is a target, I would have moved that student's seat to a different part of the room a long time ago. In addition, I would create a social studies lesson centered on bullying. I would make sure all students knew the behavior of a student who bullies and why he or she is bullying. I would provide all students with an action plan, in that lesson, instructing them on the things to do if they are ever a target. I would also solicit a police officer from the neighboring district to come to the class to discuss with students the legal ramifications of being a bully. I would set up expectations for bullying behavior and set consequences for this behavior. Prevention is key and consistency is necessary. I would also alert security and other support staff that we had a potential bullying problem so they too could be on the lookout to help protect the student being bullied.

    Circulating the classroom checking for students who E.N.G.A.G.E. themselves in small group collaborations, activities, projects, and lessons is imperative to good classroom management. Getting near to students plays such a critical role in managing behavioral situations and especially in making those interactions positive, private, and necessary. I move about the classroom throughout the day, during all activities, in order to establish proximity to address behavioral situations before they happen. Circulating the classroom makes me highly visible. In essence, I see when things aren't going well and recognize when students are off their game. It also calls heightened attention to me and my actions making it almost impossible for students to engage in inappropriate behavior within my proximity, and students never know when I will be in their proximity. By circulating the room, I am constantly out and about, and I will be able to correct inconspicuously as I monitor, observe, and teach.

Circulating the room will not prevent all inappropriate behavior from occurring. Some students will figure out how to get their "bad" where they can. However, as I walk by my student's desk, I walk past slowly enough for them to understand that I am monitoring their behavior giving constant, brief, and unspoken interactions. As I circulate, I am friendly, but not trying to make friends, as I must remain the authority. I can touch student's desks making them see I am observing their work and their actions closely. I come to class with a tool belt full of quick complementary or corrective interactions and give literal thumbs up, say "good job", and smiles often.

Additionally, I do brief stop-bys (stopping by student desks) to read and review student work. This heightens the level of engagement. For students who I know try to intimidate others, I may even pick up their papers to read them and provide them with a greater level of scrutiny that keeps them on their toes and focused on their own work instead of others. This lessens the time they have to think of new ways to bully. Sometimes, I may comment, other times I may not. Students with practiced inappropriate behavior receive more visits from me. At the same time, reading, assessing, and responding to student work in real-time are important ways to check for student understanding and showing them that I am interested in both them and their work. For students who need more attention, this quells the inappropriate and bad behavior spells they may display. The practice of circulating the classroom providing students with verbal and nonverbal interactions as well as giving complementary and corrective feedback in real-time is my classroom management tip for this case study. Because students have been taught to E.N.G.A.G.E. themselves, I ask students who are off-task how they can redirect themselves based on E.N.G.A.G.E.

Case Study 2:

Today, you have the desks in your classroom arranged especially for large classroom discussions. They're all turned in a semi-circle fashion with your seat in front of the room; clearly showing you're the moderator and a major encouragement. All-day, students have been quite enthusiastic to participate in the discussion, but in the 3rd class of the day, one student refuses to participate. You call on the student multiple times, attempting to engage him, but the student is non-compliant, answering every time with shrugged shoulders and a mumbled "I dunno." **"What is the best way to handle this situation?"**

I would first assume that this student is emotionally distraught and proceed with caution by stopping my request immediately. I would "catch" that student before he or she walks out of the classroom and ask him or her to come to my office during break time. However, a student's willingness to be open to my assistance is based on the relationship I have already built with that student. If I do not have a relationship with him or her, this is the perfect time to attempt to build one. However, my attempts to build a relationship with this student should not stop me from putting this student in the face of another staff member who has that working relationship already. I must ensure the student that he or she is NOT in trouble. This student is obviously emotionally distraught and it is my duty to dig deeper to find out why and how to help. I must recognize that an emotionally distraught student is in danger academically. He or she will not be able to learn the lessons I am prepared to teach.

Case Study 3:

Students have been instructed to begin today's assignment that requires independent reading and answering three questions to confirm comprehension. A student consistently causes disruption during the lesson. The entire class focus has been compromised and all the students are now off task. The teacher tries to ignore the students' disinterest in the lesson and teach through it. The situation has escalated and now the students refuse to return to normalcy. **What would you do to regain control in the classroom?**

First of all, I would never assign independent reading or independent work and then go to the front of the class and sit behind my desk. This action tells my students I am not really interested in what they are doing; instead, I want to isolate myself from them, so they can do whatever they want. This tells them what I want them to act inappropriately so they can regain my attention. I tell them that I am more interested in doing whatever it is I am doing at my computer or behind my desk than I am in teaching them and giving them feedback on their work.

I will always circulate the classroom making eye contact with students who have a tendency or history of being disruptive. It is usually the same students. I am of the opinion that once I enter that classroom, my role is to engage students from beginning to end. Class time is not a time for me to read independently, organize, or even grade papers. Class time is not a time, when students are present, is not a time for me to multi-task. My only objective is to engage students in various learning tasks and monitor their interactions with the work and with each other. These "housekeeping tasks are tasks for another time when students are not present.

In this case, however, I would stop the class for a few minutes, in order to get them back on task. My actions must be precise, authoritative but kind, and quick. The ultimate goal is to remove the culprit from his audience so other students can return to work. During those moments I would make eye contact with that disruptive student and remove him or her from the audience. I would quickly rethink and rearrange the seating arrangement. Next, I would give a quick pep talk and restate the instructions for the assignment and the expectation pre-established for the activity in order to redirect students to the assignment.

My verbal and nonverbal communication in this situation would be stern and authoritative. I would walk the disruptive student to the hallway for a private pep talk while positioning myself in the doorway so I can keep my eye on the rest of the class. A quick reminder of the behavior expected and a reminder of a time when the student's behavior was appropriate and in compliance will often be enough to redirect this student. When the teacher has taken the time to develop a relationship with this student this quick intervention will suffice. After the pep talk, the student would be seated in front of the classroom away from other students. At this point, I would continue circulating in my usual manner of providing verbal and nonverbal feedback while continuing to keep my eye on the disruptive student.

Case Study 4: The Math Teacher

A student shared his experience in one of his math classes, during his junior year of high school. This happened in Chicago, in what was supposed to be a "Gifted," test-in educational program. The teacher was presenting a new math concept via a slide presentation on the classroom Smartboard. The lights were dimmed, but it was not dark in the classroom. Let's pretend the name of the concept was "Condition." The teacher was explaining the concept, walking around the classroom utilizing the handheld clicker to change slides. As she was explaining the math concept she had to repeat its name "Condition," over and over. The former student stated that not too long into the teacher's presentation a male student stood up and said loudly, "Shut the (bad word) up! If you say "Condition," one more time I'm gonna knock you the _uck out (bad word)! Turn the mother (bad word) lights on, sit your bad word down behind your desk, and shut the guck up! Don't say another mother (bad word) (bad word)!"

As a result, a student turned the lights back on, the teacher sat behind her desk and did not say another word. The former student stated that the classroom didn't get very loud but the students commenced to do whatever they wanted to do, which was various different things. The former student and others were very disturbed by the situation, yet no one ever reported this or other situations like this to the administration or their parents. That day, the former student stayed behind and asked the teacher how he was supposed to learn the new concept because he needed it for his future college major. She stated to him that she would be holding after-school tutoring of that and future concepts two days per week in her classroom. It ended up being 3 days for almost as much time as the students needed. But, only the geeky students attended so it was peaceful, and didn't take too much extra time. Also, some of the smarter students did help other students, but for the most part, they just cheated on homework and tests. The teacher did not teach in the classroom anymore until the threatening student stopped attending, near the end of the semester. **How can this class be recovered and organizing instruction for active teaching and learning begin?**

Problem

The administrator had not built a relationship with the teacher, which would have established a two-way channel of communication. In doing so, the teacher might have felt comfortable voicing her concerns and the need for assistance. This teacher does not appear to have been appropriately trained in classroom management and crisis intervention in a classroom, which is integral in an at-risk environment. Classroom Management in a school where disruptive youth attend is very different from a healthy school environment.

Take Away

An administrator who works in a volatile school environment should have interventions and securities in place for a teacher, just in case they need it. This teacher should not be afraid of retaliation from the student. Also, administration in such an environment should ensure there is a behavior management support staff circulating the hallways. Classroom doors should not be closed so that the circulating behavior staff could hear what goes on in the classroom. Behavior Management support staff should be assigned to each hallway, monitoring the classrooms in their section. There should be one behavior support staff who knows this student well and has formed a relationship with him. These staff members would also be responsible for tutoring students; so, they need to have at least two years of college or a high school diploma with a high GPA and ACT or SAT score. Hiring the right people in this position is delicate and paramount.

The teacher should feel comfortable discussing the situation with the administration as well as other colleagues. This specific incident is a topic of discussion for the teacher's professional learning community. Every teacher who touches this student needs an opportunity to discuss his behavior, his academic progress, and his needs. Each teacher, including this math teacher, should have formed a relationship with this student.

This math teacher did not have crisis prevention knowledge. A simple intervention she could have applied, if she formed a relationship with him, is to remind him of a time when his behavior was reasonable or appropriate for the classroom. She could have reminded him that it was the behavior she expected from him today. However, this simple intervention will not work if a student-teacher relationship is not formed. She did not know how to respond to a crisis. She did not know how to intervene, and she had no support available to her to intervene. There should be regular ongoing review and training about how to respond to behaviourally challenged students in volatile situations.

Plus, there should be a code the teacher could use to get the circulating staff member's attention so she could have the volatile student removed. A school-wide crisis intervention plan is the first thing that should be applied with no fear. The student should be removed from the class so the teacher can teach the other students with no interruption. It is best practice to remove a disruptive student from the audience. This student could have been taught or reminded of appropriate behavior ensuring his success instead of waiting for him to disappear. More than likely he disappeared into the ranks of street gangs, then probably in prison or dead.

Lastly, no staff should touch this student to remove him from the classroom without proper training. Ongoing behavior management training of every adult in the building should happen regularly on this school campus. As an educator, I would never condone schools being a pipeline to prisons. Involving security and police is a very last resort after many other behavior support measures have been exhausted. In an environment prone to volatile student behavior or where safety is a factor, there should be a team of behavior management support staff, not security. Look as behavior support staff as mentors who have also developed professional and healthy relationships with each student to whom they are assigned. This staff member should become the student's advocate. I would assign 8-12 students to each Behavior Management support staff, depending on student backgrounds. In a larger school, I would group students and assign them a behavior management staff along with their homeroom teacher. Both of these faculty would partner to develop relationships and get to know the academic as well as personal challenges of a group of students. When situations like this are described in the math class, one of these faculty members will most likely be able to talk to this student down and get him back on track in the classroom.

Behavior management staff would also attend professional learning communities where teachers discuss specific teaching, learning, and behavior management strategies on a regular basis. In most schools, the dean or assistant principal is in charge of student behavior. This administrator would also be in charge of ongoing training for the Behavior Management support staff. They need training in crisis management, behavior, tutoring, as well as mentoring.

Case Study 5: Tolerance and Acceptance

The setting is a dual credit high school on a junior college campus in the inner city. The student population is 95% African American, 3% Hispanic, and 2% Transgendered. The classroom size is 32 students, without adequate support in the classroom. The school is known for housing challenged students with socio-economic barriers, academic deficits, and a host of social ills. One of the most pointed challenges is that of gender tolerance and acceptance, which had become a huge issue for the school. Transgender students had made numerous complaints about feeling uncomfortable and unsafe while in school. They had talked with the teacher and principal concerning bathroom visits. These students had reported being harassed while using the boys' bathroom and refused to continue using it. They requested the use of the girls' bathroom as they would feel safer. They asked to be referred to like girls and be allowed to use an empty ladies' bathroom. The teacher refused their request and said she had no authority to do so. While in the classroom, students were reluctant to interact in collaborative assignments with them. This particular day, while in the boys' bathroom, the two transgender students were jumped on by a group of boys and beaten up very badly. They had to be taken to the hospital, the boys were suspended for three days. Upon returning to school, nothing was done, to the dismay of the two transgender students. They eventually dropped out of school and refused to return. **What could have been done to circumvent the threats that impacted the culture and climate of the classroom?**

Dealing with the diverse ways in which my students learn is the major issue on which I place my focus. I see 'students' who need variant and differentiated teaching and learning. I do not see race, gender or sexuality. My concern and focus are how does each student learn? What does each student need me to do to ensure that they learn? What is the best assessment I can use to ensure individual students are learning what I am attempting to teach? What am I teaching that each student has not learned? Why? What can I do to ensure teaching and learning?

However, all students have the right to a safe learning environment. My goal is to create an environment where all my students feel safe physically, emotionally, and academically. There is beauty and power in diversity. It is my goal to be the model for teaching faculty, staff, and students to adopt an attitude of tolerance and acceptance.

Problem

The problem in this situation is that bias existed among administration and faculty. If the situation had been turned around and two boys were being bullied by the other boys and beaten up in the bathroom so badly they had to be hospitalized, what would have happened? The boys who did the bullying and beating would have had consequences. That is what would have happened. So, why weren't these consequences applied in this situation? The consequence did not fit the crime.

Takeaways

What are the consequences of bullying and fighting? If these consequences had not been established yet, then using the professional learning community model, now would be a good time for administration and faculty to establish them using restorative justice methodology. Students who did the bullying and beating would be required to repair the harm caused by their actions. Whether or not the students who were harmed were gay, lesbian, transgender, Black, White, Hispanic or other does not matter. What matters is that two students were bullied and beaten to the point of hospitalization. They were victimized and harmed. Period. According to restorative justice, the two victims and the offenders would sit in a peace circle with identified administration, faculty, and staff to discuss the situation and decide consequences for the offenders and what the offenders will do to restore the harm done to the victims. Hopefully, the results will be transformational.

Restorative justice emphasizes responsibility by holding the offenders accountable for their actions. It emphasizes the need to make amends. The peace circle will be facilitated by a certified peace circle keeper. In an environment as volatile as this behavior staff will be trained and certified as licensed peace circle keepers. As an administrator with trained behavior management staff in the building at all times, I would hope this situation could be identified, monitored, and prevented before it happened. Also, as an administrator, I would like to have known why this problem was not identified, monitored, and prevented before it blew up into a crime. This would be a justification for ongoing training and improvement of both teaching and behavior management staff. The fact that nothing was done to offenders is a huge problem for me. The fact that two students did not feel safe enough to return to school is also a huge problem for me. The incident is a crime, criminal behavior cannot continue to happen in a school where I am an administrator. Criminal behavior cannot happen in a classroom where I teach.

Transformation is the Pay Off

I aid in the transformation of the mindsets of generations in deep, meaningful, and significant ways. Many of our students are responsible for and influence others. Most are parents, care for elderly parents, and are heads of households. We get them at a perfect time in their lives when they usually have a stronger desire to improve or enhance their lives more than ever before. Though we do get some young people fresh out of high school, most of our students are those who have been out of high school for a few years or more. Many have attended the University of Hard Knocks and are now ready to do something different, to be somebody else. I relate well to my student's backgrounds. I grew up in Englewood before my family moved to yet another low socioeconomic neighborhood. I graduated from a high school in the heart of "the hood" too. I remember when I too graduated from that university of knocks, after a bad 21-year marriage, 5 children to impact as a single parent, the parting of both parents, and a bankrupt business.

I appreciate the instructors who helped me get it together and I just want to give back, to pull someone else out, and to help someone improve the quality of their lives. There are some, however; who are only attending college because they're being forced to do so by a parent, a caregiver, a governmental agency, and yes, even a parole officer. Nevertheless, that is passable, because I have a goal; my goal is to inspire even those students! When students are inspired, they learn to acquire basic skills on their own. They seek out other resources and they learn to love to learn.

A common adage states, "When you are not willing to learn, no one can help you. When you are determined to learn, no one can stop you". There is too much in life to learn for learning to be complete; there are so many students who have not learned. When they learn to love learning, they literally begin to teach themselves. My teaching has become transformational as my students change me daily. They make me better at what I do. My students learn to love to learn and I reaffirm my love for teaching.

The payoff for building trust with students, planning meticulously, and providing specific feedback benefitted me, my students, and their future teachers as well. The personal relationship I build with students spills over into my faculty learning community, and other departments on campus as well. My students are least likely to be a challenge for support staff advisors and other faculties. Many times, they will stop me in the hallway for semesters after they completed my courses telling me how what they learned from me benefitted them. My students are more likely to give new teachers and teachers stuck in lecture mode the benefit of the doubt. The real payoff is spoken in these student testimonials.

> *"Ms. Yisrael, I would like to thank you for all your hard work and dedication, put into my education and making English 96 Arc course a success for me. I was very stressed about coming back to school after so many years, but you managed to make it comfortable for me with your wonderful teaching skills. I look forward to registering for the English 101 fall semester with you."*

> *"Thank you, Prof Yisrael, What I thought I knew was correct, and what I knew was reinforced. I appreciated your academic diligence and professionalism. I will feel better prepared when I need to write and publish of which I know I will be doing plenty. Again, I appreciate your support."* English 102

> *"I learned a lot out of your class. Thank you for expecting a lot from me. You made me believe I could reach your expectations and I could not disappoint you."* English Arc 96

> *"You understand exactly how to get the most out of your students. I have a better understanding of essay writing and the research process because of your class. Keep up the good work."* English 102

> *"Thank you again for all your help and how you encouraged us throughout the school year. I appreciate everything you taught us and I learned so much from this class. Your help made learning great and because of this I am prepared for English 101. I want to thank you again for all your help. It really meant a lot to me."*

> *"Your syllabus is well constructed and I fully understand the system of the*

projects and assignments. If I need help I'll ask you during your office hours. Other than that, you do an excellent job." English102

"I would suggest students take Professor Yisroel's class because she provides a lot of information on Brightspace that helps her students pass, she inspires her students to learn with consistency, and she follows up on student learning behaviors when some of us get out of pocket and cause a distraction." English 101

"I was so afraid when I came to your class. I was afraid I wouldn't fit in. I was afraid I would not be able to do the work. I was afraid I could not read fast enough or understand enough of what I read. I was just afraid. By the end of the the first week of class, many of my fears just disappeared." English 96 Arc

"This is a letter of admiration to my professor, who is very focused and driven. She is the most inspiring, constructive lecturer at Kennedy-King College. I took her English composition class and African American Literature class. This professor makes learning enjoyable yet challenging. The way she can open up scholars so they can absorb information is impressive. Professor Yisrael knows how to reach her students, and show them ways of wisdom that other instructors would not even attempt to. I just want to say the style of educating she imparts, is the winning formula. " Literature 121

"Professor Yisrael, You are a fantastic professor because you really truly connect with your students. You speak on topics that are relevant to your students. You give rich assignments that give myself and my classmates passion and fire. We are eager to do the assignments. You are truly experienced in the culture. The civil rights movement, contemporary arts era, black arts movement are all topics I've learned so much about since I've taken your course. I am someone who really truly loves to write and I feel like your courses give me the essentials and tools it takes to perfect my craft. You inspire me as a student Professor Yisrael as you do the rest of your students. Thank you." Literature 121

"I have learn more about Black history in your Protest Poetry class than I ever did in any history class. I expected this course to be an easy A. I did get an A but it was not easy. I did not realize I needed the challenge . I really appreciate you for that." Protest Poetry 111

"I'm in my second year at Kennedy King College. I have had the pleasure of taking several of Professor Yisrael courses. I took her English, Poetry, and African American Literature courses. If I see her name in the schedule for a class I need I will register. . Her teaching style is unique, and my writing has improved tremendously under her guidance. I'm able to examine, analyze, and evaluate literary works. In addition, my ability to brainstorm and put my ideas on paper is not as much of a challenge anymore. Professor Yisrael consistently challenges students to learn and grow, and she is passionate about teaching. I'm more confident in my writing and capabilities because Professor Yisrael provided me with key skills I can use not only just in college but beyond." Literature 121.

According to a 2013 survey by Gallup, teaching ranked as one of the healthiest of professions. Teaching makes real teachers happy. We get the extra hugs, even from successful adult students. Occassionally, we get simple token gifts and appropriate celebrations. It is a great profession, if one is a life-long learner. Teachers constantly have cause to do further research and learn from it. We constantly have reason to take another class ourselves. We love telling our success stories at faculty development workshops and peer functions. We are encouraged by the bragging rights. More than anything else it feels simply amazing being in the grocery store and be greeted by a previous student and their family with a beautiful smiles and testimonies about how you inspired them to improve the quality of life for themselves and their families. Most of love it when a student who we taught got that great job, earned an advanced degree, and make good money. The payoff is simple appreciation and knowing we made a difference to someone's life. These two things make us forget we are so very underpaid.

11
Educator's Growth Plan

Understanding the impetus of becoming an effective change agent, effective educators are encouraged to join the initiative to pick up the gauntlet to further this educational reform. Considering the construction of affective (feelings) as well as effective (successful) relationships, it is imperative to create sustainable, systemic channels of communication. Teachers and students, as well as all invested in the education of today's students, must commit to bridging gaps and forging ways for effective communication, collaboration, emotional awareness, relevant and sustainable learning while making every minute count. Therefore, for every plan, there must first be a plan, we must 'plan the plan'. Our goal is to change pedagogical practices with a more in-depth fix on 'at risk' behaviors as opposed to looking at 'at risk' students; for all students are 'at risk' for failure, if not give adequate or appropriate needs to move forward. Our theoretical lens is through the 'whole student' principles predicated upon social-emotional and emotional intelligence tenets, and restorative practices. The Educator's Growth Plan acts as a guideline to safeguard the appropriateness and relevance of teaching today's 21st Century learner. It is a hope that these reflections and activities will empower educators who empower our youth.

Reflections for Becoming Better at Developing Projects for Inquiry-Based Learning.

Brainstorm a list of projects you want to plan for your students. Then create a Project Development Worksheet for each project. Next, decide which project you will plan and implement first and use the E.N.G.A.G.E. planning process to complete your planning.

1. _____
2. _____
3. _____
4. _____
5. _____
6. _____
7. _____

Inquiry-Based Instruction
Project Development Worksheet

Project Topic/Title: _____

Purpose: Why is this a good topic for your students? How would it benefit them?
_____
_____
_____
_____

1. What are the skills to be mastered within the project?

2. Will the project support the Common Core standards? Which? How?

3. Is the project relevant to the students' interests and issues?

4. How can the project support collaboration and team-building among students?

5. How can the project support collaboration and team-building among other courses and faculty?

Reflections & Activities to Make Every Minute Count

Activity 1:

Video Search: Conduct a YouTube search of these video titles. Analyze the videos, one at a time.
- GIRL SNAPS AT TEACHER FOR NOT TEACHING CLASS!!!
- Student wins an epic argument
- Student Destroys Feminist Teacher with Facts.
- High School Student Goes Off On Teacher About Education!
- teacher gets told

Exercise: As you watch the videos, observe the behavior of the disruptive student, peers, and the teacher. Imagine you are the teacher and this is your classroom.

- Observe what happened. Describe it.
- What went wrong in the first place?
- How did the class get to this?
- Reflect upon a few strategies regarding how the teacher could get the disruptive student as well as her peers back on task.

Activity 2:
1. What resonates with you about Making Every Minute Count?
2. Have you ever worked at a site where participation in a professional learning community is encouraged? Was it beneficial? How? Or Why not?
3. Can reflections help you to grow and become more reflective?
4. How have you been influenced to be more reflective in your instructional practices?

Activity 3:

Reflective teaching is, therefore, a means of professional development that begins in our classroom. Take daily notes or write in a journal. Analyze and evaluate these reflections to make changes and improvements to your teaching practices. If students are misbehaving, look at yourself and your behaviors more than your students. Ask yourself: (Keep notes or write your responses in a journal).

- What am I doing?
- When am I doing it?
- Why am I doing it?
- How effective is it?
- How are the students responding?
- How can I do it better?

Activity 4:

1. Think about the value of reviewing and reflecting on your best classroom management practice. Think about how your best practice allows your students to better learn. What do you already do that you find beneficial and effective?

2. Think about one of your weaknesses in the area of classroom management. How could you improve this strategy to best ensure you are successful in its implementation?

3. Form a faculty learning community with 3 or 4 of your peers. Set aside a weekly or biweekly time to share your reflections with them. On a regular basis, collect information regarding everything that goes on in your classroom. Identify then reflect upon your own practices and your underlying beliefs about them. Reflect upon behavior problems as well as learning challenges as they occur.

4. Share your best practices with your professional learning community. Observe one another's classroom and provide feedback. Decide what you will observe ahead of time.

Activity 5:
Take away: When making every minute count, teachers should:

- Establish expectations for conduct and civility to encourage appropriate participation.
- Plan all exercises and activities to draw attention to issues and content you feel are most critical.
- Introduce the activity and explain the learning benefit.
- Control the time cost by giving students a time limit to complete the task.
- Make EVERY MINUTE COUNT.
- Collaborate with 3-5 colleagues to complete the plan using the ENGAGE process.

Exercise: The goal of the activity is to have participants leave the workshop with 4 complete ENGAGE action plan worksheets.

1. Share 3 sample ENGAGE action plan worksheets with participants. Discuss each item in one worksheet.
2. Have participants collaborate with a small group of 4 to 5, have participants generate a list of common activities in which they engage students in their classroom?
3. Have participants collaborate with their group to complete one E.N.G.A.G.E. action plan for one of the activities on the list?
4. Have participants collaborate with a partner to complete another E.N.G.A.G.E. action plan for an exercise on the list?
5. Have participants work independently to complete 2 E.N.G.A.G.E. action plans for two more exercises on the list?

E.N.G.A.G.E   Action Plan Worksheet

Teacher_____ Class_____ Date_____

Exercise
1. Describe the exercise. 2. What is the activity? 3. What is the expected product?

Nurture
1. How will the teacher nurture students during the exercise? 2. How will the teacher ensure they receive the support and help they need to successfully complete the exercise? 3. How do students get the teacher's attention to get their questions answered? 4. What do students do in case they have to wait to get the teacher's response to their questions? 5. How do students get the motivation to complete the exercise successfully? 6. How does the teacher create opportunities to build students up?

Grade
1. How will the exercise be assessed? Is a rubric needed?
2. What are the expectations for grades using a grading rubric?
3. How can students earn an A?
4. How can students earn a B?
5. Why might a student earn a C for the exercise?
6. Why might a student earn a D for the exercise?
7. Why might a student earn an F for the exercise?
8. What formative assessments will the teacher use to improve the exercise?
9. What online tools will be needed to monitor and assess the exercise?

Action
1. What are acceptable actions and behaviors for the exercise?

2. What actions and behaviors show students are participating responsibly and fully?

3. How long will the activity last?

4. How should students manage their time?

5. What online tools will students use to complete the activity?

6. How are students expected to participate in the exercise?

7. What should students do when they are done?

Genuineness
1. What is honest?
2. What is integrity?
3. What is true?
4. What is forthright?
5. What is plagiarizing?
6. What is cheating?

Exchange
1. Can students talk or exchange ideas with a partner?
2. Or group
3. For how long?
4. How often?
5. For what reason?

References

Angelo, T. A., Cross, K., & T. (2006). *Classroom assessment techniques*. Jossey-Bass: San Francisco.

Bain, K. (2004). *What the best college teachers do*. Cambridge, MA: Harvard University Press.

Bean, J. C. (2011). *Engaging ideas: The professor's guide to integrating writing, critical thinking, and active learning in the classroom*. Hoboken, NJ: Wiley.

Bereiter, Carl & Scardamalia, M Learning to work creatively with knowledge. 2003.

Beaudry, J. S., & McCafferty, A. S. (2018). High-impact teaching that creates assessment-literate learners. Thousand Oaks, CA: Corwin.

Biggs, John. (2006). "Enhancing teaching through constructive alignment". Department of Educational Psychology. University of Sydney. Australia.

Biggs, J. B. (2001). Teaching Across Cultures. Student Motivation, 293-308. doi:10.1007/978-1-4615-1273-8_14

Boscolo, P., & Mason, L. (2003). Topic Knowledge, Text Coherence, and Interest: How They Interact in Learning from Instructional Texts. The Journal of Experimental Education, 71(2), 126-148. doi:10.1080/00220970309602060

Brooks, J. G., & Brooks, M. G. (1993). In search of understanding: The case for constructivist classrooms. Alexandria, VA: Association for Supervision and Curriculum Development.

Christakis, D. A. (2016). Focusing on Smaller Adverse Childhood Experiences. JAMA Pediatrics, 170(8), 725. doi:10.1001/jamapediatrics.2016.0392

City Colleges of Chicago. Academic Affairs (2013). *The Talents of Teaching for CCC Faculty*.

Costa, A. L., & Kallick, B. (2018). Learning and leading with habits of mind: 16 essentials characteristics for success. Alexandria: Association for Supervision and Curriculum Development.

Cox, R. D. (2011). The college fear factor: How students and professors misunderstand on another. Cambridge: Harvard University Press.

Equipped for the Future (2004). Teaching/Learning Toolkit. Learning logs.
http://eff.cls.utk.edu/toolkit/tools_learning_logs.htm

Harris, N. B. (2018). The deepest well: Healing the long-term effects of childhood adversity. London, England: Bluebirds Books for Life.

Text Complexity: Raising Rigor in Reading (9780872074781): Nancy Frey, Douglas Fisher, Diane Lapp: Books. (n.d.).

Fullan, M. (2008). The Six Secrets of Change. San Francisco, CA. John Wiley & Sons Inc.

Jensen, E., & McConchie, L. (2020). Brain-based learning: the new paradigm of teaching. Thousand Oaks, CA: Corwin Press.

Johnson, S. (n.d.) Faculty strategies for promoting student learning.
http://www.csudh.edu/titlev/learninglog.htm

Hattie, J. (2011). Visible Learning for Teachers. doi:10.4324/9780203181522

Hiebert, E.H. (2009), Using multiple sources of information in establishing text complexity. (Reading Research Report No. 11.03). Santa Cruz, CA Text Project and University of CA, Santa Cruz.

Kirkpatrick, S. (2007). Assessing Student Learning: A Common-Sense Guide? By Linda Suskie. Teaching Theology & Religion, 10(2), 114-115. doi:10.1111/j.1467-9647.2007. 00329.x ts/reflective%20journal_LL/index.html

Lefoe, Geraldine. (1998). "Creating Constructivist Learning Environments on the Web: The Challenge in Higher Education". Centre for Educational Development and Interactive Resources, University of Wollongong, Australia.

Marzano, R. J. (2005). School leadership that works. Alexandria, VA: Association for Supervision and Curriculum Development.
Merriam, Sharan B. Third Update on Adult Learning Theory. San Francisco: Jossey-Bass, 2008. Print.

Merriam, S. B., Ross-Gordon, J. M., & Imel, S. (2008). Third update on adult learning theory. San Francisco: Jossey Bass.

Moss, C. M., & Brookhart, S. M. (2009). Advancing formative assessment in every classroom: A guide for instructional leaders. Alexandria, VA: Association for Supervision and

Curriculum Development.

Munin, A. C. (2012). Color by number: understanding racism through facts and stats on children. Sterling, VA: Stylus Pub.

Nordin, A. M., Hilib. H., & Ghazali, Z. (2011) Strengthening internal (study) Communication: A case of communication satisfaction in an organization. European Journal of Social Sciences – Vol. 24., Number 419.

Northouse, P. G. (2007). Leadership: theory and practice (4th ed.). Thousand Oaks, CA: Sage

O'Connell, T., & Dyment, J. (2006). Reflections on using journals in higher education: A focus group discussion with faculty. Assessment & Evaluation in Higher Education, 31(6), 671-691. doi:10.1080/02602930600760884

Paskevicius, M (n.d.). Conversations in the cloud: The use of blogs to support learning in higher education. http://bluelightdistrict.org/assets/SharedBlogs_2010_v5-completeFinal.doc

Richardson, Virginia (1997). Constructivist Teacher Education: Building a World of New Understandings. Bristol PA: The Falmer Press.

RMIT University. Study and Learning Centre. Melbourne, Australia (2006). Reflective journals.

Perloff, R. (1997). Daniel Goleman's Emotional intelligence: Why it can matter more than IQ. [Review of the book Emotional intelligence. D. Goleman]. The Psychologist-Manager Journal, 1(1), 21-22.

Relationship of Childhood Abuse and Household Dysfunction to Many of the Leading Causes of Death in Adults Felitti, Vincent J et al. American Journal of Preventive Medicine, Volume 14, Issue 4, 245 - 258

Robert Emmerling - Member Emotional Intelligence Consortium. (n.d.). Retrieved from http://www.eiconsortium.org/members/emmerling.htm

Shockley-Zalabak, P. S. (2006). Fundamentals of Organizational Communication. Boston, MA: Pearson Education, Inc.

Solomon Amy, MS, OTR (2007). Faculty Development Workbook, Module 6: Classroom

Management for the Adult Learner. Clifton Park: Delmar Cengage Learning.

Sparks, G. M. (1988). Teachers attitudes toward change and subsequent improvements in classroom teaching. Journal of Educational Psychology, 80(1), 111-117. doi:10.1037/0022-0663.80.1.111

Stevens, D. D., & Levi, A. J. (2005). Introduction to Rubrics: An assessment tool to save grading time, convey effective feedback and promote student learning. Stylus Publishing: Sterling, Virginia.

Stevens, D. D., & Levi, A. (2013). Introduction to rubrics: An assessment tool to save grading time, convey effective feedback, and promote student learning. Virginia: Stylus.

Strong, R. (1995). Strengthening Student Engagement: What Do Students Want. Princeton Junction, NJ: Association for Supervision and Curriculum Development.

Wachtel, T., (n.d.) What is Restorative Practices, Restorative Justice International
http://www.iirp.edu/what-is-restorative-practices.php

Wang, Q. (2009). Designing a web-based constructivist learning environment. Interactive Learning Environments, 17(1), 1-13. doi:10.1080/10494820701424577
Weimer, Maryellen. "A Few Concerns about the Rush to Flip." *Effective Teaching Strategies for the College Classroom*. Web. 18 Nov. 2014. <http://www.facultyfocus.com/>.

Wachtel, Ted. (2012). "Defining Restorative". International Institute for Restorative Practices.

Wiggins, G. P., & McTighe, J. (2008). Understanding by design. Alexandria, VA: Association for Supervision and Curriculum Development.

Writing to learn learning logs (n.d.).
http://www.wku.edu/3kinds/mfllmpg.html#Independent%20Study